Secrets and Keys of the Born Again Kingdom

By Adrian D. Hay

© **Adrian D Hay 2018**

This book is dedicated to all my family.
May the Lord bless them and keep them.
May the Lord make his face to shine upon them,
and be gracious to them.
May the Lord lift up his countenance upon them,
and give them peace.

Preface

This book is particularly aimed at people who, like myself, have been born again and need to know what to do with it. Often we find ourselves as Born Again Christians but with no real direction and guidance on what to do or what to say. I spent a good year just reading the Bible, watching God TV and seeking out information on this seismic event that had just happened in my mind and in my life. I write this book to help others understand what is going on and to help people walk the Christian life that they should. My local vicar didn't much speak to me for the whole year after I had had my experiential rebirth, apparently because she wanted to see if I fell away from Christ. My aim is to write a book that helps you stay in Christ and understand the things that the Church doesn't tell you in a normal Sunday service. Along with my roots in the Church of England are quite a few inserts from the Pentecostal movement because I felt a little different from the majority of Christians in the congregation. When you come to faith, you are part of the body of Christ so you are going to want to be with other Christians. They are your family now and it is up to you whereabouts in that family you live.

We are all on this journey with Christ. Some walk a long road and some, like I did, get a sudden boost and grace which transforms us supernaturally. This is not necessarily because we are extra special, but because we needed it. I am yet to speak to a born again Christian who did not need salvation and is not grateful for it. I suggest you read on......

Contents Page

INTRODUCTION

*F*or 40 years of my life, God and Jesus were pretty irrelevant to me. I was brought up in a Christian household with Christian parents and church on Sunday. I went to Sunday school and Cubs and Scouts and Venture Scouts and was a server in church which was what I thought I was just supposed to do. I presumed I was Christian. As I grew older, other things took over my life like chasing girls, alcohol, nightclubs and reckless behaviour. Seemed like a natural progression to me. At just sixteen I was involved in a serious road traffic accident but survived with a double broken leg and head injuries. Over the next few years, I had to relearn a lot of things. I had an idea I had survived for a reason.

I went on to get a degree and trained as a teacher. During my first job as a secondary teacher in greater London, I had a teaching assistant who told me he was a spiritualist and that he got quite a strong sense of my inner being. He described how he once lowered his hand over a pupil who told him that he was touching his head long before he actually was. He explained that we are all spirits living this life to learn certain things and sometimes our spirit extends beyond our body. He gave me an example that a spirit might want to learn what it is like to be poor so it lives a poor life. I thought that this was very interesting.

Years later a friend of mine, who was living in his uncles very old and central London flat, called me late at night, pleading with me to drive into central London to collect this panicking friend who had just seen a ghost. I was so tired and really didn't' want to make the effort but because of his alarmed sincerity, I did. Things started to add up.

A few years later, I was at party somewhere completely different. There was a woman who could allegedly speak to the dead and indeed told one man how his dead son was doing. I went to talk to her and the strange thing was that she was instantly scared of me and I had no idea why.

I reached 40 years old and although I had an amazing birthday, things soon went downhill. I was made redundant, I split from my fiancée who kept custody of my baby daughter and I was just plain lost. A friend of mine told me to find something to believe in so I decided to get to the bottom of things and find out what all these religions are praying and worshipping.

I investigated and spoke to people of all different religions and they all had something in common, a higher being. A while later and probably because I was living opposite to a vicarage, I went on the Alpha course. This was my life changer.

By Adrian D. Hay

∞ ∞ ∞

CHAPTER ONE Being saved

*L*et me quickly tell you what happened to me. I was on the Alpha course, a course designed to lead non-Christians to Christ. I had been persuaded to go on it by my local vicar who had previously tried a few times but without success. I stopped refusing and I went on it to be the devil's advocate, in a sense. I was arguing and trying to disprove everything I could but really searching for the answers I needed to prove or disprove this Christian God. One week, I wasn't going to attend so the vicar gave me a Nicky Gumbel book to read whilst I took my daughter to my mums for a long weekend. It was on Tuesday that I thought that I'd better read some of this book because that vicar would probably be asking me questions. That was the only reason I read the book. So I read and I read and I found that I just couldn't stop.... It was so engrossing. Then, around midnight, I can only describe it as being hit in the stomach by lightning as I was filled with joy and light but with nobody to share my happiness with because they'd gone to sleep upstairs. I went to my bedroom and since I knew how to pray from when I was a child, I got down on my knees and shut my eyes. They quickly opened and I tried shutting them again. I could not keep my eyes closed because of the intensity of the white brightness – it was painful. With my eyes shut, I could not bear to look at the light because it was beyond bright and it was everywhere. I opened my eyes and confused as I was, shut them again but only to come into this bright light again which had no sign of fading. If there is anything to confound the mind, then this is it. It was too painful to keep trying to shut my eyes and I later understand how the Apostle Paul became blinded. I have no idea how I got to sleep, but I woke at 7.30am chanting "spread the word" and "he is coming" just like a madman.

After breakfast, I went outside and everything looked so beautiful. The trees, the houses, the birds.... Literally everything was beautiful. It started raining and that was beautiful too. And that was the restart of me. My own daughter, young at the time, must have sensed a change because she was asking who I was, and stating that she didn't know me.

I understand that many people have been born again and I do know lots of others, so I know that being born again is fact and not fiction. Some say that my experience was extraordinary but I think the extent of the experience relates directly to how much we need it or how far off track we have drifted. It was very weird and I still don't completely understand it but I get the idea.

As my vicar explained, suddenly I am transformed into "one of them". I'm one of those strange people that go to church and like to read the bible and sing halleluiah songs and hug everyone, whether you know them or not. But I'm getting used to it, bit by bit. I enrolled on church courses at the Cathedral and I'm getting certificates as I'm learning more and more about this man they called Jesus. I'm also watching a lot of God television and particular worship leaders that I have been led to watch, sometimes by waking up sharp at three in the morning or once by a butterfly coming in my house and settling behind the television which prompted me to put it on. By the way, once you are born again with God, expect some crazy things to happen.

The following chapters are the things that I have learned. Be very aware that this is my experience and everyone is different and your experience may be completely different or yet to come. We do have something in common though, and that is Jesus Christ.

I also learned that it is important to read the Bible. The Bible tells the whole story of the world from the creation story of Adam and Eve all the way through to the end. In fact, this book is a history of the world but one of the few history books that's written before everything has taken place. By Bible, I don't just mean the New Testament, it's the Old Testament too. There's an old adage that says that the New Testament is in the Old concealed, the Old is in the New revealed. That is so true.

I used to live in the world and didn't think much about God or no God. I was a consumer, consumed by the things around me. I was fascinated with women, nightclubs and alcohol, money and even drugs. Sounds normal but, in fact, my life wasn't going well at all. I had ended up in a situation where I was truly lost and I was clutching at anything that would give me hope. They say that reaching the end of yourself becomes the start of Him. Reaching the end of myself pretty much sums things up. I didn't have a clue what to do with my life or where to go. I was filled with anger and I was potentially dangerous. I used to lift heavy weights at the gym, getting energy and strength from the hate I had for people. It was as if I was at war with the world and I was gearing up to take it on. I researched many different faiths and even satan who I thought would be useful because through my work, I was seeing a lady that I really shouldn't have been seeing. I wanted to be with her full time so I summoned satan and guess what.... an immediate text telling me that she had been kicked out of the family home. It was too much of a freaky coincidence to be anything other than true. Looking back, I am so glad that God stepped in.

And now I think I went soft. I'm called to honour God. Today I hear people talk about Jesus in public. More often than not it's using His name as a swear word, and especially when things don't go the right way. For me, I now love to hear his name, whatever the circumstance but as Christians, we love and honour and worship him like no other and there's a reason for that.

You might start to realise that God is an amazing God and although we can't see him or touch him, we know that he is there. We have accepted him and we are his children. This is why we are sons and daughters of God and we should live our life, doing things in the name of Jesus. It is not wrong to let everybody know what your faith is. You are receiving from him through his blood and you receive the honour that comes with the blood.

1 John tells us that because we have the spirit of God, we are like Jesus because Jesus had God in him.

13 This is how we know that we live in him and he in us: He has given us of his Spirit. 14 And we have seen and testify that the Father has sent his Son to be the Saviour of the world. 15 If anyone acknowledges that Jesus is the Son of God, God lives in them and they in God. 16 And so we know and rely on the love God has for us.

I've shared my testimony with a few people but probably not enough. At one point I even had my testimony published on the web site of Holy Trinity Church, Brompton, England – the home of the creator of the successful and well recommended Alpha course, Nicky Gumbel. Sharing your testimony is vital to the advancement of the kingdom. Sometimes it is nice to keep it comfortably locked away but as Jesus would tell you, faith comes by hearing. Therefore, you have to spread the faith by telling. Romans 10 tells us this.

14 How, then, can they call on the one they have not believed in? And how can they believe in the one of whom they have not heard? And how can they hear without someone preaching to them? 15 And how can anyone preach unless they are sent? As it is written: "How beautiful are the feet of those who bring good news!"

As a Christian, it becomes your duty to be a storyteller or a light of God for others to see. Not everybody has mind bending conversions to Christianity but if you are born again then something happened to change your direction in life. You can talk to people about this and the joy that it brings you. I could win the top prize in the national lottery and still say that the best thing that happened to me was being born again or coming to Christ. It really is no small thing to be accepted into God's family and have an eternal future ahead of you. It's a lot better than facing eternal damnation with no idea what is going to happen to you. There are many people in this position and they don't even know for sure that God exists.

There are many accounts of Jesus and what he did in the bible. The bible is a collection of 66 books written by around 40 authors and they didn't write this for entertainment. They wrote it for you and me to learn, live and to spread the good news. It is actually better described as over-the-top good news in that we have a future after death. The soul lives on.

∞ ∞ ∞

CHAPTER TWO – Obedience

*I*t became so undeniable that there is a God. There is someone or something more than what we see, hear, smell and touch. I once heard it mentioned that Christians think that they have an invisible friend and in a way, that's the truth. But that is just like gravity. You can't see gravity but if you walk off a tall building, you'll soon learn about it. God exists too!

Around the world, there are many religions and they mostly focus on something extra or supernatural which would be beyond nature that we know (the natural). All religions have got one thing right. There is a higher being and hopefully you have recently discovered this and the God that leads you to salvation.

I was on holiday in Madeira and was in the capital Funchal with my young daughter and we were standing around in the sun. I can remember it quite clearly because the next thing that happened was the guy next to me said "Find three people to talk to about me". So I turned but was aghast to see that there was nobody there and it definitely wasn't my daughter and besides, it was a male voice. I kind of knew it was God so I nervously approached four people starting with a nearby policeman and had a brisk casual conversation about God. It was like the pass-the-parcel game where you are keen to pass it on. I asked my daughter if she had heard the voice since she was right next to me. But no, she hadn't. It felt like I was going a bit mad, once more!

As a born again Christian there was a lesson in there that we've got to understand. He is the great almighty God who created all things and when he tells you to do something, just do it. I have found that he doesn't always make sense and he doesn't always ask you to do things that you want to do, but I think this is your opportunity to learn the servant mentality. Another example of God speaking to me is when I see someone else's litter on the floor and I hear "pick it up". It drives me crazy and to be honest I really don't like it, but I do it. In airports, in shops, in schools.... He tells me to pick rubbish up and because he is the boss, I do. Later I find out that obedience is the number one characteristic that God is looking for.

Another thing I learnt was to leave things alone until God changes them or tells you to change them. In other words, don't do or change a thing until he tells you. Remember that you may have just given your life to God so it's important not to take it back. When God is ruling in your life, you handed over control to him. Imagine being on a bus and the driver lets you drive it but is constantly trying to get back behind the wheel... that is not a safe scenario for the passengers!

You may not hear God speak or maybe that's for later. I have spoken to many Christians who have never heard God speak and that's ok. He often speaks to us in many different ways. My vicar used to tell me that God spoke to her using the weather. And I thought that I was going mad!

It is worth noting that God prepares you for his tasks. God has a task for you and as Jerimiah 29:11 says,

"For I know the plans I have for you," declares the Lord, *"plans to prosper you and not to harm you, plans to give you hope and a future".*

So I was picking up litter and this was training me for obedience. I also went through a long period of not working which meant that I had to claim benefit and ended up on the "work scheme". For much less than minimum wage, I found myself working in an old stately home serving food to various needy groups. At one point I was so upset about doing this that I stood in the kitchen and cried out "Why Lord?". The reply came in an audible voice. He said "I want you to see how all things work together". A lesson I'll never forget.

If you are born again and I hope that you are, there is something very important I want to say. As soon as I was born again, the first thing I needed to know was how to reject it. How to become not born again. Why? So that I didn't lose this "gift", this very precious gift. And the answer I found is to reject the holy spirit. Therefore, NEVER reject the holy spirit. You might swear curse or whatever but just do not reject the holy spirit or he might reject you. You've perhaps been saved from quite a messy situation, so I suggest that it is very handy to know how not to backslide. But it is not even backsliding... it is giving up that one chance of salvation for your soul. Don't even mess about trying to do it. There is someone who will try and get you to do it and he's talked about more later in the book.

I remember sitting next to a man in church who was all for Jesus but told me that he didn't believe in hell. Well, nobody talks about Hell more than Jesus. It is a real place and is worse than scary. I have a friend that has had countless visitations of heaven. Not me. But I did go to hell. It was similar to being on the moon but black with molten lava and creatures that were like those from the film "Alien", the ones with the long shiny heads. The thing that struck me the most was the intense feeling of fear and absolute loneliness as if I were the very last human and I was prey for all the other creatures. Suffice to say, I don't want to go there again and I really don't want anyone else to either. If this is really the case and I suspect that it is, we do not have a clue what we are facing after death and it is so important to get people saved. I knew hell would be bad, but had no idea what bad really meant. I've spoken to people about heaven versus hell and they've even told me that they're happy taking their chances. Not me.

Can you loose birth?

Interestingly, to go to heaven, Jesus tells Nicodemus that you must be born again. He wasn't just talking to Nicodemus but this is for everyone. Let's have a look at John 3.

Jesus Teaches Nicodemus

3 *Now there was a Pharisee, a man named Nicodemus who was a member of the Jewish ruling council.* [2] *He came to Jesus at night and said, "Rabbi, we know that you are a teacher who has come from God. For no one could perform the signs you are doing if God were not with him."*

[3] *Jesus replied, "Very truly I tell you, no one can see the kingdom of God unless they are born again."*

[4] *"How can someone be born when they are old?" Nicodemus asked. "Surely they cannot enter a second time into their mother's womb to be born!"*

[5] *Jesus answered, "Very truly I tell you, no one can enter the kingdom of God unless they are born of water and the Spirit.* [6] *Flesh gives birth to flesh, but the Spirit gives birth to spirit.* [7] *You should not be surprised at my saying, 'You must be born again.'* [8] *The wind blows wherever it pleases. You hear its sound, but you cannot tell where it comes from or where it is going. So it is with everyone born of the Spirit."*

[9] *"How can this be?" Nicodemus asked.*

[10] *"You are Israel's teacher," said Jesus, "and do you not understand these things?* [11] *Very truly I tell you, we speak of what we know, and we testify to what we have seen, but still you people do not accept our testimony.* [12] *I have spoken to you of earthly things and you do not believe; how then will you believe if I speak of heavenly things?* [13] *No one has ever gone into heaven except the one who came from heaven—the Son of Man.* [14] *Just as Moses lifted up the snake in the wilderness, so the Son of Man must be lifted up,* [15] *that everyone who believes may have eternal life in him."*

[16] *For God so loved the world that he gave his one and only Son, that whoever believes in him shall not perish but have eternal life.* [17] *For God did not send his Son into the world to condemn the world, but to save the world through him.* [18] *Whoever believes in him is not condemned, but whoever*

does not believe stands condemned already because they have not believed in the name of God's one and only Son. ¹⁹ This is the verdict: Light has come into the world, but people loved darkness instead of light because their deeds were evil. ²⁰ Everyone who does evil hates the light, and will not come into the light for fear that their deeds will be exposed. ²¹ But whoever lives by the truth comes into the light, so that it may be seen plainly that what they have done has been done in the sight of God.

John Testifies Again About Jesus

²² *After this, Jesus and his disciples went out into the Judean countryside, where he spent some time with them, and baptized. ²³ Now John also was baptizing at Aenon near Salim, because there was plenty of water, and people were coming and being baptized. ²⁴ (This was before John was put in prison.) ²⁵ An argument developed between some of John's disciples and a certain Jew over the matter of ceremonial washing. ²⁶ They came to John and said to him, "Rabbi, that man who was with you on the other side of the Jordan—the one you testified about—look, he is baptizing, and everyone is going to him."*

²⁷ *To this John replied, "A person can receive only what is given them from heaven. ²⁸ You yourselves can testify that I said, 'I am not the Messiah but am sent ahead of him.' ²⁹ The bride belongs to the bridegroom. The friend who attends the bridegroom waits and listens for him, and is full of joy when he hears the bridegroom's voice. That joy is mine, and it is now complete. ³⁰ He must become greater; I must become less."*

³¹ *The one who comes from above is above all; the one who is from the earth belongs to the earth, and speaks as one from the earth. The one who comes from heaven is above all. ³² He testifies to what he has seen and heard, but no one accepts his testimony. ³³ Whoever has accepted it has certified that God is truthful. ³⁴ For the one whom God has sent speaks the words of God, for God⁽ⁱ⁾ gives the Spirit without limit. ³⁵ The Father loves the Son and has placed everything in his hands. ³⁶ Whoever believes in the Son has eternal life, but whoever rejects the Son will not see life, for God's wrath remains on them.*

He we see Jesus explain to Nicodemus that born again people get access to the kingdom of God. A kingdom that you cannot see normally in the world. Access to a kingdom which allows you to operate in a way which is just like Jesus. When Jesus was baptized with the holy spirit, the holy spirit was seen as a dove coming out of the heavens. This same holy spirit is upon those who are born again. We have the potential to do the same things that Jesus did!! How awesome is that? It is, but we end up doubting and questioning our ability so we don't always walk in His ways.

Nicodemus is thinking in physical or natural terms and is perhaps imagining a baby coming out of the mother. But Jesus is not talking about rebirth in this sense. He is talking about spiritual rebirth which is a completely different thing to physical birth. Spiritual rebirth is having your mind opened to the spirit world, the world of the Holy Spirit. Imagine that you have an airplane that you use to go on vacation or even to go to work. You do this without any problems for a lot of years. Something happens and you find out how to turn the radar on and suddenly you are aware of all the other airplanes in the air. In a not so dissimilar way, this is what I think it is like to become aware of the spirit world.

But Jesus tells us that you must be born of the spirit to have eternal life. At one point, I really was wondering if eternal is something I want. Most people aren't lucky enough to go through life without problems and so a life of eternal problems doesn't sound like the perfect Christmas present. But do not worry, eternal life isn't eternal life as it is at the moment. God created the world and everything in it. This would be it. But, as the story goes, an angel called Lucifer (interesting name choice for the evil Lucifer Morningstar from Superman) who is the most beautiful angel has a change of heart and wants the power and glory that God has and because of this gets ejected from heaven and roams the earth in an eternally super annoyed way, trying to upset Gods' world. Why doesn't God just kill Satan? That would make sense to me, but God has created these angels with eternal life and with free will (humans too). God cannot go back on his word, no matter what. *– Why not?*

God now has a plan which involves, as I put it, cherry picking. God has a new world and people are almost chosen to be Christians and lined up for this new world. God has created this new world for us *? not true* to enjoy eternal life and enjoy it without Satan and all the bad things that he brings. Imagine that. Only good things happen. Wow.

So if you are saved, your name will be in the Book of Life or book of destination which is a list of people destined for heaven or the world to come. This is talked about in the last book of the Bible, The Book of Revelation. So if you are Christian, your name is in the book of life and you are safe, right? Well, apparently, your name can be *No! ?!* blotted out. Forgiveness gets your name in the book of life and holiness keeps you in. Holiness is living a holy life that is acceptable to God. Holiness is being blessed and the Beatitudes give us a good idea of who is entitled. We also have the 10 commandments but I didn't realise what they actually meant.

The Beatitudes

On the sermon on the mount, everything is explained by Jesus and the beatitudes are also given. The name "beatitudes" is Latin for "happiness".

Jesus teaches us in Mathew 5:

5 Now when Jesus saw the crowds, he went up on a mountainside and sat down. His disciples came to him, ² and he began to teach them.

The Beatitudes

He said:

³ "Blessed are the poor in spirit,

for theirs is the kingdom of heaven.

⁴ Blessed are those who mourn,

for they will be comforted.

⁵ Blessed are the meek,
for they will inherit the earth.
⁶ Blessed are those who hunger and thirst for righteousness,
for they will be filled.
⁷ Blessed are the merciful,
for they will be shown mercy.
⁸ Blessed are the pure in heart,
for they will see God.
⁹ Blessed are the peacemakers,
for they will be called children of God.
¹⁰ Blessed are those who are persecuted because of righteousness,
for theirs is the kingdom of heaven.

¹¹ "Blessed are you when people insult you, persecute you and falsely say all kinds of evil against you because of me. ¹² Rejoice and be glad, because great is your reward in heaven, for in the same way they persecuted the prophets who were before you.

Jesus then goes on to enlighten us about the 10 commandments that Moses brought.

Salt and Light

¹³ "You are the salt of the earth. But if the salt loses its saltiness, how can it be made salty again? It is no longer good for anything, except to be thrown out and trampled underfoot.

¹⁴ "You are the light of the world. A town built on a hill cannot be hidden. ¹⁵ Neither do people light a lamp and put it under a bowl. Instead they put it on its stand, and it gives light to everyone in the house. ¹⁶ In the same way, let your light shine before others, that they may see your good deeds and glorify your Father in heaven.

The Fulfilment of the Law

¹⁷ "Do not think that I have come to abolish the Law or the Prophets; I have not come to abolish them but to fulfil them. ¹⁸ For truly I tell you, until heaven and earth disappear, not the smallest letter, not the least stroke of a pen, will by any means disappear from the Law until everything is accomplished. ¹⁹ Therefore anyone who sets aside one of the least of these commands and teaches others accordingly will be called least in the kingdom of heaven, but whoever practices and teaches these commands will be called great in the kingdom of heaven. ²⁰ For I tell you that unless your righteousness surpasses that of the Pharisees and the teachers of the law, you will certainly not enter the kingdom of heaven.

Murder

²¹ "You have heard that it was said to the people long ago, 'You shall not murder, and anyone who murders will be subject to judgment.' ²² But I tell you that anyone who is angry with a brother or sister will be subject to judgment. Again, anyone who says to a brother or sister, 'Raca,' is answerable to the court. And anyone who says, 'You fool!' will be in danger of the fire of hell.

²³ "Therefore, if you are offering your gift at the altar and there remember that your brother or sister has something against you, ²⁴ leave your gift there in front of the altar. First go and be reconciled to them; then come and offer your gift.

²⁵ "Settle matters quickly with your adversary who is taking you to court. Do it while you are still together on the way, or your adversary may hand you over to the judge, and the judge may hand you over to the officer, and you may be thrown into prison. ²⁶ Truly I tell you, you will not get out until you have paid the last penny.

Adultery

²⁷ "You have heard that it was said, 'You shall not commit adultery.'[e] ²⁸ But I tell you that anyone who looks at a woman lustfully has already committed adultery with her in his heart. ²⁹ If your right eye causes you to stumble, gouge it out and throw it away. It is better for you to lose one part of your body than for your whole body to be thrown into hell. ³⁰ And if your right hand causes you to stumble, cut it off and throw it away. It is better for you to lose one part of your body than for your whole body to go into hell.

Divorce

³¹ *"It has been said, 'Anyone who divorces his wife must give her a certificate of divorce.'*[f] ³² *But I tell you that anyone who divorces his wife, except for sexual immorality, makes her the victim of adultery, and anyone who marries a divorced woman commits adultery.*

Oaths

³³ *"Again, you have heard that it was said to the people long ago, 'Do not break your oath, but fulfil to the Lord the vows you have made.' * ³⁴ *But I tell you, do not swear an oath at all: either by heaven, for it is God's throne;* ³⁵ *or by the earth, for it is his footstool; or by Jerusalem, for it is the city of the Great King.* ³⁶ *And do not swear by your head, for you cannot make even one hair white or black.* ³⁷ *All you need to say is simply 'Yes' or 'No'; anything beyond this comes from the evil one.*

Eye for Eye

³⁸ *"You have heard that it was said, 'Eye for eye, and tooth for tooth.'* ³⁹ *But I tell you, do not resist an evil person. If anyone slaps you on the right cheek, turn to them the other cheek also.* ⁴⁰ *And if anyone wants to sue you and take your shirt, hand over your coat as well.* ⁴¹ *If anyone forces you to go one mile, go with them two miles.* ⁴² *Give to the one who asks you, and do not turn away from the one who wants to borrow from you.*

Love for Enemies

⁴³ *"You have heard that it was said, 'Love your neighbour and hate your enemy.'* ⁴⁴ *But I tell you, love your enemies and pray for those who persecute you,* ⁴⁵ *that you may be children of your Father in heaven. He causes his sun to rise on the evil and the good, and sends rain on the righteous and the unrighteous.* ⁴⁶ *If you love those who love you, what reward will you get? Are not even the tax collectors doing that?* ⁴⁷ *And if you greet only your own people, what are you doing more than others? Do not even pagans do that?* ⁴⁸ *Be perfect, therefore, as your heavenly Father is perfect.*

Jesus redefines the commandments. All the commandments that I thought I was safe from breaking, I now knew that I had broken. Furthermore, he tells us that if you break one commandment then you have broken the lot. And I thought that the original Jewish people had a hard time with all the 600 plus laws that that had to abide by.

Did you know that you must overcome temptation to inherit eternal life because only the pure get into heaven? This is written in Revelation, chapter 21 verse 27.... Nothing impure will ever enter it, nor will anyone who does what is shameful or deceitful, but only those whose names are written in the Lamb's book of life which is another title to that book of destination.

Psalm 34 tells us: *15 The eyes of the Lord are on the righteous, and his ears are attentive to their cry; 16 but the face of the Lord is against those who do evil, to blot out their name from the earth.*

The good news is that God offers both forgiveness and holiness. So we have a chance and this also explains why people go to confessional and why people bother to repent. We can do wrong things and repent to bring us back to holiness. You have to do it with sincerity, there's no other way. If anyone's name is not written in the book of life, they are hell bound and that is not funny.

So now you are in Christ, all of a sudden Sin seems to be the "in thing". You hear "sinners are bad" or "don't sin" - there is nothing worse than sin according to Christians.

I've lived a long time and I have never had a problem with sin. In fact, being born again brings about something previously unknown to me and a new sensation called "sin consciousness". I feel there should be a whole chapter on this. Sin is critical to the life of a Christian. When a Christian sins, you need to repent (ask for forgiveness) and you are back to being holy. This is how it works but only if you mean it. I love it when a friend of mine says "Lord, I repent of everything I've done wrong" .... I'm not so sure that catch-all's work but I've done it myself a few times. Anyway, in John 8:34 Jesus tells us that whoever sins become a slave to that sin.... For example, you might look at pornography and before you know it you can't stop... in effect, it controls you. How would you deal with this? Ask for forgiveness from the father and reject all the images from your mind so that they are not lurking and enticing you. Temptations come around time after time, and you have to deal with them. Reading the word of God in the bible often helps you to realign your mind. I've never been any good at knowing what to read in the bible so I have resorted to reading from the front to the back and it's not quick, but at least I don't miss anything!!

The book of proverbs also tells us that you <u>must</u> confess your sins.

"Whoever conceals their sins does not prosper,
but the one who confesses and renounces them finds mercy."

If you have sinned, it is important to realise your sin and repent and ask the Father for forgiveness. In old testament times, goats and sheep were sufficient for the paying of the sin but since Jesus took the cross in payment for all our sins, our Father can hand out forgiveness to the genuine asker. This is how you effectively keep a clean sheet.

It is wise not to think of God in human terms because he is much more than this. He is wiser, he is much more intelligent and he is the boss. Some things just won't make sense to you but I can assure you that if you are a Christian, then these things that don't make sense will be part of his plan in some way that you can't yet see... but you will.

∞ ∞ ∞

CHAPTER 3 Loyalty

*P*salm 34 verses 8 and 9 gives us good advice about the Lord.

Taste and see that the Lord is good; blessed is the one who takes refuge in him. Fear the Lord, you his holy people, for those who fear him lack nothing.

I can remember myself asking a number of people why I need to be scared of the lord because it does say to *fear* the Lord. It doesn't mean to be scared of the Lord but to respect him and honour him. He is the almighty God who created us, the animals, the trees, the world, the universe and basically everything so he really is worth praising and worshipping. He is the creator and when you have transgressed from not knowing him to having a relationship with him, then you have accepted him as the Lord Almighty and inherently, the boss. You don't often keep your job if you go to work and tell the boss what to do so once you have given your life to Christ, let him lead and remain loyal.

Don't forget that Satan is after you or after your position as a child of God, but don't let him have it. He is nothing to be scared of because you are mightier that you might realise. You are a child of the almighty which means having complete power and your father is omnipotent which means that he is everywhere. As a child of God you should have the same power and authority as Jesus! Jesus never addressed the devil as Sir. You must never forget that He that is in you is greater than He that is in the world. This can be found in the bible under 1 John 4:4.

I love how it is that thousands of years ago, people wrote the new testament bible which was really an account of what happened when God came to earth. Why did God come to earth? Because mankind had got things wrong and they were not honouring God in the right way and being the people that God intended them to be. When God the creator, created the human race, he gave them free will but they misused this. Before I was born again, I had the mentality of "have as much fun as you can because you're not here forever". This would be similar to people pre (and post) Christ and the root of the problem. This is most definitely Satan driven, but then again, he does rule this world and blind people to the truth of God. The only way God could manage to get the message to us humans would have been to come to earth as Jesus and teach us and show us. It feels like the old adage of "sometimes you just can't get the staff" when you bear in mind that he had the Priests, Prophets and Seers (Visionaries) throughout the old testament who were translating God for the people.

In the old testament there were a lot of battles and fighting and it wasn't peaceful times. Similarly, once you are of Christ, there seems to be a big opposition working against you or there certainly does for me. Sometimes obvious opposition and sometimes sly but it is opposition and it is spirit led but not the spirits that we like.

It is essential to remain loyal to the Lord. I hate to hear about Christians who have fallen away and I implore you to keep looking up, with a focus on Jesus and don't worry about things of this world and especially who is in it. Psalm 56 says

When I am afraid, I put my trust in you.
4   *In God, whose word I praise—*
in God I trust and am not afraid.
   What can mere mortals do to me?

And it is correct. You were born of the flesh and now of the spirit. Your life does not end at death but continues way beyond. At worst, someone might kill you but you have eternal life through Jesus Christ which means that you continue to live but elsewhere. I now understand why Christians look so happy, it really is amazing when you realise that you are "safe", no matter what.

I was praying for a relative of mine who was interested in Christianity but not saved, and she had an experience during the night where she left her body and her spirit was flying amongst the trees with other spirits. Now, I'm not saying that that is a normal Church of England Christian experience but it certainly has relaxed her on-earth attitude, knowing that there is more to life than what we know. Another lady from my local church told me how she looked down on her body in the operating room of a hospital and yet another friend told me how he had left his body and looked down on himself getting on with life which would indicate that we are operating on a series of repetition loops that we've learnt if we can continue without our spirit. Fascinating proof of the spirit.

You could say that Jesus died to prove that death is not the end of all things. He proved without doubt that you can't kill him. Jesus resurrected himself. He got up from crucifixion and kept on telling the same story about God. He told us that we can have life in abundance if we follow His ways and that there was a future for us, and this was after death. This is no ice breaker, it demolishes the common way of thinking, and with a sledgehammer.

All this information is written in the bible and the more you read it, the better off you are. No-one told me this when I was struggling to read and understand the King James bible, but it is sound advice to find a bible version that is easier for you to read. Personally I like the New International Version and I also read the English Standard Version because it flows very well. I started reading the King James because I thought it would be closest to the original but I have come to realise that understanding is more important, and God will guide you. In my initial hunger and passion to read the bible, I just read it because I thought it was the spirit in me that needed to read it and so I wasn't too concerned with understanding. But I am now.

From the beginning of the Bible, you will see that the great almighty God, created the world and everything in it, with words. He literally spoke things into existence. The animals, the flowers, the trees, the valleys, the mountains, the grass, the people.... He literally spoke everything into existence. It took me a while to get my head around this but I can now believe it. The bible emphasises the power of the Word and the power of the Tongue. Hebrews 11:3 tells us that God spoke the world into being by the power of His words. That's right, words have power. You can make things happen with words. We all know that you can buy houses, you can get jobs and you can attract the opposite sex with the right words. The power of Words is not to be underestimated and a careful use of words will help you advance in life. For us Christians, the most important words are those written in the bible. They contain the meat for life and this abundant life that we are entitled to.

It took me a long time to guard my mouth and the words that I speak. The bible refers to the tongue in proverbs 21 and says that the tongue has the power of life and death and those who love it will eat its fruit. The tongue is like the serpent in the garden of Eden who can run ruin if allowed to. Have you ever said something you didn't mean to say? Don't forget that no matter how great words can be to build things or edify them, they can also hurt people and demolish things. What can you demolish with words? A person's confidence for example. It is too easy to say the wrong thing to people and that is why in the morning I often bind my tongue to be a Christian tongue in the name of Jesus Christ. Jesus simply spoke to a fig tree and it died. Jesus said that you can move mountains with your words. Some people believe that these are actual physical mountains but I rather think that these are the obstacles in your life. For example, finding employment can become such a massive task that it becomes a mountain in your life. Jesus teaches us to talk to that mountain and others like it and move them out of our way. As a child of God, there should be nothing stopping us living a full life.

It is amazing what you can do with your words. I was fortunate enough to be able to buy a nearly new car which was top of the range. I really liked this car and everything was working perfectly in the car. It was much better than the previous car. And then you get a little niggle. A little something that takes the edge off the joy that you have. The CD player stopped working whilst I was driving. It would not turn on. I stopped driving and turned the car engine off for a few minutes and then tried again. After a few attempts, the CD player was working again. A few weeks later, however, I was driving on the motorway and the CD player stopped working. I pulled into the services, turned my engine off and I waited. It took a few attempts before the CD player started working again. When I returned home, I knew that I had a problem and booked the car into the local main dealer for diagnostics. Before the allocated appointment time arrived the CD player stopped working again. This time, however, I remembered what I had read in a brilliant book called "Seven Secrets to Power Praying" by Jane Glenchur. Here she gave testimony that even when electrical things go wrong, you can talk to them. The CD player should be working fine but it isn't. I commanded the CD player to work and I bound any demons or works of the devil in Jesus' name. I didn't keep my appointment at the garage and have never had another problem with the CD player. I used words and the problem was solved.

There is a risk in buying things second hand. All I am saying is that you do not know who had what you purchased before you and you certainly do not know what their spiritual history is. If for example, a previous owner was a devil worshipper then anything I buy from them has the potential to cause me trouble. The fact is that more often than not; you just don't know. Therefore, I prefer to buy brand new if I can and if I can't, I will be praying over purchases beforehand and praying over the purchased goods to rid them of any demonization. There's no point in me thinking there's something wrong with my Christianity when I'm surrounded by demonic influence. Similarly, if I go into someone's house and there is a statue of Buddha or another idol, I can't help but cringe. It's not Christian so don't expect it to bring you good luck.

Another example where I have used words, comes a few days after my salvation. I was by a pool under the trees and I wanted to pray in silence. I was massively devoted and wanted only time with God. I could hear cars, I could hear geese, I could hear the wind in the trees and I commanded it to stop in Jesus's name. Very freakily I had stillness and silence instantly. It was very powerful and my young daughter felt and noticed this too. Not a sound. It is still a weird event to this day. It made me think of when Jesus calmed the storm. There is power in the name of Jesus.

This was when I was just born again and I felt that everything was fresh and I was completely pure and not "dirtied" by the things around me. Soon after, people start saying "you can't do that" or "you're not good enough" or "miracles are from thousands of years ago" or "I don't really believe in Jesus" and somehow it affects you and as you go to work and deal with all sorts of issues, you seem to dirty or spoil this initially pure faith that you had. And it is a shame. I have heard an account of being in church when a guy comes in convinced that he is Jesus. He was so convincing that the people in the church were thinking "well maybe....". He might have been a "nutter", nobody knows, but what I do know is that this is exactly how I felt by the pool. I felt as if I was Jesus and I had His holiness and His power and it was perfect. Worldly things started to kick in and my sense of pure holiness diminished somewhat. It wasn't that my ability had diminished but my faith had taken a beating. You need the word of God plus faith to have power.

Many of the TV evangelists are exclaiming that you need to renew you mind. And I think that you do. You need to try and stop thinking about worldly things. These are the things that everyone craves for in life. More money, a faster car, a bigger house, security, nicer food, better clothes and the list goes on. Some of these are great and I certainly lived craving those things in the past. I can remember my cousin calling me Mr. Gadget because I had to have the latest electronic device or phone. But as a Christian, your whole focus has to be changed. Remember when I spoke about getting as much fun out of life as you can before you die? Well now it's a case of pleasing God and being transformed into a new you, a you that is Holy enough to be able to enter into the new world that God lives in and wants you to live in too.

But how do you do this? You have to make God the focus of your mind which is not easy. Soon enough many distractions enter your life and I have found that working a job pretty much takes your mind off God and onto what you're doing. We do however know that work is good according to the bible. The Lord likes us to work and good work is apparently as good as worship as long as you are not working against God, doing something that he would be displeased with.

Some times on your journey, you will be tested, you will come across blockades, you will feel that you are useless, you will feel that there is no point but you must keep on going. Some of this is God testing you and the other, well, that's the devil trying to cause problems. It sounds a bit far-fetched but I recall that when I was making sense of the whole Jesus thing, I did liken it to the game of Dungeons and Dragons becoming a reality (similar to Game of Thrones). Suddenly, you are actively playing in an all too real game of survival. You are not fighting against the man in the fish and chip shop or the attendant at the swimming pool or your doctor or your teacher, but against demons and devils and witchcraft and sorcery which can be anywhere.

On your journey, it is important to regularly talk to God and we do this mostly through prayer. You are a son or daughter of God and it is paramount that you talk to your God or you will have little or no protection against the forces that are against you. You could just pray to God and give him your list of what you want and then wait to see whether it happens. I have found that a better prayer life starts with worship. Notice that a lot of what we might call "Jesus songs" do this by praising God by how great he is, how amazing he is and how awesome he is. This is a relationship you are having with the Lord and therefore some praise and worship will really help with this relationship. Marriage is also a relationship but when the partners stop appreciating and praising each other, it becomes dysfunctional and we all know where that leads. You have a marriage relationship with God, with Jesus, and good communication keeps it going as does appreciation and worship. If I had a partner who constantly gave me a to do list and nothing else, I doubt I would want to stay in that relationship and I'm willing to bet that there are plenty like me. With a little thought, most people know how to run a good relationship and they have to apply this to their relationship with God.

We are also taught to be serious about prayer. In James 5,

"Elijah was a human being, even as we are. He prayed earnestly that it would not rain, and it did not rain on the land for three and a half years. Again he prayed, and the heavens gave rain, and the earth produced its crops."

Notice that Elijah is described as a human being who is no different to us. It is stating that we can pray for things to happen.... We can stop the rain or stop the wind just as I once did at the Pool. It is not about who we are but it's about who God is and the power that we have access to through the sacrifice of Jesus Christ.

It is important to realise that born again Christians are spirit led people. We are led by the holy spirit and spiritual things are just as real as physical things. God is a spirit and his kingdom is a spiritual one.

God is out of time. He doesn't operate in the same world as us and I don't even think he has a watch. I am not saying that God doesn't know about time but that his time is different to ours and therefore his sense of urgency is also different to ours. If you ever want something to happen quickly, you might have to pray earnestly about it otherwise God might just take his own time about doing things.

The world that we live in was created from a spiritual God in a spiritual world which tells us which existed first. Jesus was a spirit before he became flesh. He was definitely flesh as Luke explains in Luke 24 36:44 as Jesus returns to the disciples:

36 While they were still talking about this, Jesus himself stood among them and said to them, "Peace be with you."

37 They were startled and frightened, thinking they saw a ghost. 38 He said to them, "Why are you troubled, and why do doubts rise in your minds? 39 Look at my hands and my feet. It is I myself! Touch me and see; a ghost does not have flesh and bones, as you see I have."

40 When he had said this, he showed them his hands and feet. 41 And while they still did not believe it because of joy and amazement, he asked them, "Do you have anything here to eat?" 42 They gave him a piece of broiled fish, 43 and he took it and ate it in their presence.

Notice that that they had the opportunity to touch Jesus and check that he was of flesh. Jesus was also hungry and eating fish which showed his human fleshy nature. As a side, it is good to note that it was not only the famous "doubting" Thomas who was unsure about it being the real Jesus, because in verse 38 Jesus asks them why doubts rise in their minds.

There is an important lesson in here for you and I. People were starting to doubt. Look at Peter when he walks on water in Matthew 14:22-33.

²² Immediately Jesus made the disciples get into the boat and go on ahead of him to the other side, while he dismissed the crowd. ²³ After he had dismissed them, he went up on a mountainside by himself to pray. Later that night, he was there alone, ²⁴ and the boat was already a considerable distance from land, buffeted by the waves because the wind was against it.

²⁵ Shortly before dawn Jesus went out to them, walking on the lake. ²⁶ When the disciples saw him walking on the lake, they were terrified. "It's a ghost," they said, and cried out in fear.

²⁷ But Jesus immediately said to them: "Take courage! It is I. Don't be afraid."

²⁸ "Lord, if it's you," Peter replied, "tell me to come to you on the water."

²⁹ "Come," he said.

Then Peter got down out of the boat, walked on the water and came toward Jesus. ³⁰ But when he saw the wind, he was afraid and, beginning to sink, cried out, "Lord, save me!"

³¹ Immediately Jesus reached out his hand and caught him. "You of little faith," he said, "why did you doubt?"

³² And when they climbed into the boat, the wind died down. ³³ Then those who were in the boat worshiped him, saying, "Truly you are the Son of God."

Did you see in verse 31 where Jesus said "Why did you doubt?". Doubt circumvents success. When I was initially born again I could make things happen like the quietening of the wind but the longer I stayed in the world, the more doubt I had and this, I suggest, is the key problem with walking a walk of faith and replicating Jesus. Worry is also a problem and worry is practically atheism where you start disbelieving that everything is alright despite having God on your side. I feel that belief in God needs to be narrow minded and 100%.

It makes sense in Ephesians 6:12, when Paul writes

"For our struggle is not against flesh and blood, but against the rulers, against the authorities, against the powers of this dark world and against the spiritual forces of evil in the heavenly realms".

As I mentioned earlier, God is in charge. There is no better way to say this. Even Job 36:11 says this.

He makes them listen to correction and commands them to repent of their evil. 11 If they obey and serve him, they will spend the rest of their days in prosperity and their years in contentment. 12 But if they do not listen, they will perish by the sword and die without knowledge.

Now this is the Old Testament and some people think that only the new testament applies because Jesus wasn't around in the old Testament. The whole of Christianity is formed around the trinity. The trinity is the godhead of God, Jesus and the Holy Spirit. This has always been and always will be and we can easily see that at least two parts of the Godhead were present in the Old Testament. Still, some people often find the new testament easier to understand. This can be because they are written in different times and in different languages with different cultural understandings. The Old Testament was written in Hebrew which was the sacred language of God's chosen people and one that focusses on context. The New Testament is written in Greek which is a completely different language with a different focus and is more similar to the way we communicate in English.

This could be why people prefer different testaments. Some do not believe that Jesus was the Messiah and therefore adhere to the Old Testament and discount the New. The Old Testament was written by the people of Judah or the Jewish people. Jesus was a Jew who did not change his name or his appearance away from Judaism. Jesus studied the Old Testament and so that says that there is nothing wrong with the Old Testament. Imagine reading a text that you know that Jesus has read himself. To me, this is really exciting. Also, from our brief look at the commandments, we see that Jesus didn't want to change the commandments in the old testament but He changed our understanding of them. Essentially, he made it harder or more likely impossible to live and keep the commandments without God.

If we are not of the flesh but of the spirit, then we do not belong to this world but are from the next world or from Heaven. A common saying is that "we are in the world but we are not of the world". It is good to remember that you are different and important to know it. Lustfulness belongs to the world and this is everything from sex to cars to the latest televisions. This lust or materialism is not good because it takes you away from the God. By the way, things that are inherently Good are from God and things that are inherently Evil are from the Devil. Is it by coincidence that they are both one letter different?

Is being Christian safe and cool? In some circles, yes. I've heard it said that if they didn't like Jesus, why would they like you? It might be good advice to buddy up with some Christian friends where you can talk openly about your faith, especially when you're not in church. It is important that you have some support for your faith. We can all slip and feel distant from God so having others of similar faith to bounce off, really helps. These are your brothers and sisters in Christ. 1 John 3 states that

Do not be surprised, my brothers and sisters, if the world hates you. *14 We know that we have passed from death to life, because we love each other. Anyone who does not love remains in death.* *15 Anyone who hates a brother or sister is a murderer, and you know that no murderer has eternal life residing in him.*

This links back to Jesus' teachings about the 10 Commandments,

Also, satan has a strategy to win a certain amount of souls a week and you have to make sure that you are not one of them by spending time in prayer and reading the bible and having fellowship with other Christians. He tries to convince you that you are not of God and that you are not loved. Every time he does this, just remember that God gave his only perfect son to the cross, for you. God surely loves you.

And it had to be Jesus on the cross. Revelation 5 tells us that no man in heaven or on earth can open the book of redemption.

Then I saw in the right hand of him who sat on the throne a scroll with writing on both sides and sealed with seven seals. ² And I saw a mighty angel proclaiming in a loud voice, "Who is worthy to break the seals and open the scroll?" ³ But no one in heaven or on earth or under the earth could open the scroll or even look inside it. ⁴ I wept and wept because no one was found who was worthy to open the scroll or look inside. ⁵ Then one of the elders said to me, "Do not weep! See, the Lion of the tribe of Judah, the Root of David, has triumphed. He is able to open the scroll and its seven seals."

Jesus is the Lion of the tribe of Judah and he could open the book of redemption which would effectively provide the escape route from earth to heaven. Jesus was the only one. This is a massive reason why Jesus should be worshipped and praised. He literally saved all our lives.

By Adrian D. Hay

∞ ∞ ∞

CHAPTER 4 Royalty

S
ince we are born again believers in Christ, we have established that we belong to God and that we are not of this world but we belong to the world to come (or we belong to heaven). Romans 8:16 tells us this.

14 For those who are led by the Spirit of God are the children of God. 15 The Spirit you received does not make you slaves, so that you live in fear again; rather, the Spirit you received brought about your adoption to son ship. And by him we cry, "Abba, Father." 16 The Spirit himself testifies with our spirit that we are God's children. 17 Now if we are children, then we are heirs— heirs of God and co-heirs with Christ, if indeed we share in his sufferings in order that we may also share in his glory.

We are therefore sons and daughters of God. This is surely good news. We have been adopted into Gods family and that is great. But is it the end? No I don't think so. We may have royal blood but we are starting a development process that will equip us for the next life. We are being tested and refined to prove that we are worthy. 1 Peter 1-3 puts it like this:

Praise be to the God and Father of our Lord Jesus Christ! In his great mercy he has given us new birth into a living hope through the resurrection of Jesus Christ from the dead, 4 and into an inheritance that can never perish, spoil or fade. This inheritance is kept in heaven for you, 5 who through faith are shielded by God's power until the coming of the salvation that is ready to be revealed in the last time. [6] In all this you greatly rejoice, though now for a little while you may have had to suffer grief in all kinds of trials. [7] These have come so that the proven genuineness of your faith—of greater worth than gold, which perishes even though refined by fire—may result in praise, glory and honour when Jesus Christ is revealed. [8] Though you have not seen him, you love him; and even though you do not see him now, you believe in him and are filled with an inexpressible and glorious joy, [9] for you are receiving the end result of your faith, the salvation of your souls.

I can't say that I'm fond of tests or exams but the end result is so valuable that it must be done. God is in control so accept what is happening to you and at all costs, keep your faith.

Don't be down hearted if you find yourself thinking of the wrong things or even doing things that you know you shouldn't. Shake it off and repent. All this is temporary. If God has started his work on you, he is very much committed to finishing. How long it takes is up to you, in a way. And we all get distracted with the things around us. I try and read the Bible everyday but I don't always manage to. I'm still human, after all.

Walking in the spirit and binding and loosing sounds quite strange. They say that as a Christian, you are not of this world, but you are on it. This is a familiar and well used saying of many evangelists and it is similarly said in John 15:19. You are entering into combat in this spiritual world you have entered, and it works like this. Anything you come across that is worthy of being in heaven or should be in heaven or possibly is, you loose it. Examples here would be the spirit of generosity or the spirit of hospitality. Things that are definitely not of heaven, you bind. A lot of this spiritual warfare takes place inside your head in the realm of thoughts. If a voice tells you to push someone in front of a car, you might bind that voice or that spirit (as we all know that the voice comes from the evil one). What I find quite useful is to bind Satan every day and first thing in the morning. Tying him up frees us to get on with our business, unhindered. Sometimes you do this and still things go wrong and keep going wrong. Again, you bind Satan. No one else is causing your problems.

It is interesting to note that another way to deal with false thoughts in your head is to reject them. So, if I start thinking about earthly sexy women but not my partner, I might say… "I reject those thoughts in Jesus' name". If I don't, these thoughts will increase until they become so tempting I can hardly resist. Rejecting the thought clears my mind and removes any associated feelings. It allows me to continue my life with a clear mind. It is similar to clearing the cache on a computer.

You don't need to be controlled by anything other than Jesus. This can be anything from pornography to nicotine. I'm sure that they are all tools of the devil but you are of Christ and so we must resist them until they are no longer desired. Notice that Jesus says to resist the devil and he will flee. Similarly, resist temptations, and they will flee. In the desert, Jesus resisted the temptations of the devil and notice how the devil didn't just flee. No, he tried another temptation. And if he can do this to Jesus, then he's more than likely to try with you.

Matthew 4 describes how Jesus is tested in the wilderness:

4 *Then Jesus was led by the Spirit into the wilderness to be tempted by the devil.* *2 After fasting forty days and forty nights, he was hungry.* *3 The tempter came to him and said, "If you are the Son of God, tell these stones to become bread."*

4 Jesus answered, "It is written: 'Man shall not live on bread alone, but on every word that comes from the mouth of God.'"

5 Then the devil took him to the holy city and had him stand on the highest point of the temple. *6 "If you are the Son of God," he said, "throw yourself down. For it is written:*

"'He will command his angels concerning you,
and they will lift you up in their hands,
so that you will not strike your foot against a stone.'"
    ⁷ Jesus answered him, "It is also written: 'Do not put the Lord your God to the test.'"
    ⁸ Again, the devil took him to a very high mountain and showed him all the kingdoms of the world and their splendour. ⁹ "All this I will give you," *he said, "if you will bow down and worship me."*
    ¹⁰ Jesus said to him, "Away from me, Satan! For it is written: 'Worship the Lord your God, and serve him only.'"
    ¹¹ Then the devil left him, and angels came and attended him.

Notice what Jesus said to the devil. He said "Away from me, Satan! For it is written: 'Worship the Lord your God, and serve him only.'". You can say this too!

One night I woke and it was pitch dark. In the corner of the room I saw a small cretin of a man standing there looking at me. I instantly knew that something wasn't right and felt unnerved. Panicking, I exclaimed the above quote and this demonic being disappeared.

As a born again, you need to be ready for these little attacks from the enemy. You might be royalty in Jesus's eyes and in fact you are, but the devil doesn't respect this and tries to steal all that you have. He obeys your command because as soon as you say "in Jesus' name" you are talking as Jesus and the devil is plain scared now. I have used this command of Jesus quite a few times so I suggest that it is definitely worth memorizing.

Sometimes during life, thoughts come into your head. I might be using the computer to research books and the thought comes into my head to look at a beautiful woman or play a game. This is obviously a distraction and so I need to get rid of this thought. I do this by rejection. I simply say "I reject this thought in the name of Jesus". As you might expect, the thought disappears and my mind is again clear. Another thought will soon appear, but we'll deal with that when the time comes. Clearly, this is the devil trying to upset what you are doing and change your focus onto things that he wants to entrap you with. It is his sneaky way of capturing your mind in the hope that your soul will soon follow. The problem is when you don't reject these thoughts and many times you might not even be aware enough to realise what is truly happening. Soon enough, there's been quite a few tempting thoughts and you are very tempted to do something. It might be to smoke or to look at pornography or to hit somebody or something else. But there is a way out.

I was driving my daughter to her friends and it was raining. I was so annoyed with people driving slow and I was calling them names and being completely unholy. She made me aware of my behaviour and I knew myself how wound up I was getting. She put a Hillsong worship song on in the car and they were singing about Jesus. I knew the song but I wasn't bothered. Eventually, I annoyingly dropped her off and then realised what was happening. So many little things had built up inside me that I had become overbearingly distraught and this was not from God, it was devil tactics. You may have come across this yourself and might say that you're just in a bad mood or having a bad day. As I had learnt in a Pentecostal church, I turned the music down and roared, imitating a lion. I roared as loud as I could, imagining that I was the Lion of the tribe of Judah. This shatters the works of the enemy. I actually did it a few times and then felt the peace of the Lord which is a calmness like no other. You know, the one that passes all understanding. It's such a relief to clear your head from the stress and anxiety and worry caused by that devil. I have to also tell you that you can also clap your hands to break these devil chains but I like to roar like the Lion of Judah (another name for Jesus). It's not a soft pretty clap but a hand hurting clap that shows that you mean it. Similarly, the roar needs to be full volume and as loud as you can – a proper roar. On my own in the car is the best place for me to do this. The fact that it works, again proves to me that there is more to life than the natural (the things that we see, hear, touch and smell).

None of the above is relevant if you don't remember who you are. As a son or daughter of God, you can become Jesus just by commanding things in his name. That is your big ability, as a Christian. And you have to use it. Be an active Christian and deal with the devil or he'll start dominating and that is not supposed to happen. There is a war going on in heaven and it has been like that for a long time. So, I'm wondering why would I want to go to heaven when there is a war going on? And then I find out that there is more than one heaven. There is the highest heaven where God and Jesus lives and where I definitely want to be. This is referred to as the third heaven. There is evidence of this in 2 Corinthians 12 where Paul talks about it.

"I know a man in Christ who fourteen years ago was caught up to the third heaven".

Then is the second heaven where the warfare of good and evil occurs and then the first heaven which is where we live and above us and in Acts 1, it describes looking up into the heavens.

As a born again Christian, you are going to have trouble. You may have come from a life where not everything was perfect. I was once a doorman and remember a guy saying "We've all got a past", and he was right. We do all a have a past and we've probably done things that, if we stood in the courtroom before God and was questioned, we would be ashamed and we wouldn't be allowed in. The good news and it is exceptionally good news, is that we can safely put all that behind us. Forget about it and start afresh in a life where we can live truly Christian lives and if and when we do slip up, we can go to the Father and ask for repentance and get it. The devil will remind you of your past and the reasons why you are not entirely genuine but that doesn't matter because you are now one with Christ and you carry his righteousness and not your own. When he does remind you of your past, don't forget to remind him of his future! You have the best big brother to lean on and that is Jesus!

It is also worth noting that there is nothing in the natural world that can touch your spirit. Truly you are a spiritual being and your mirror is now the bible. The more you read and absorb the bible, the more like you will become until you reflect it. A spiritual life is a really good life but as soon as you believe that you are physical and of the world then that's when problems start such as sickness. ?!

One of my favourite comments is that we are spirit beings and we have an earth suit which is our body. We wear it until we are finished with it. Then we will be with the Father in Heaven. It would be wise for you to focus on this and cast away all fear and doubt. Everything was going well for Adam and Eve in the garden of Eden until doubt set in. Be positive and focus forward on your end promise of eternal life with the Father.

When you are born again you have the spirit of the Lord inside of you. This is the Holy Spirit. When God looks at you he sees his perfect spirit. Do not lose sight of this and forget about thinking that you're not good enough. You are good enough, you are perfect in His eyes. Nothing else matters. *Yes, so we no longer have to earn it!*

∞ ∞ ∞

CHAPTER 5   *Heaven on earth*

J heard someone ask that if heaven is so great then why aren't all the Christians killing themselves. When promoting Christianity, one man said to me that he didn't want to go to heaven, because it would be full of Christians! That gives us a clear picture of the lack of understanding of this world. I think that a heaven full of devoted Christians would be like Christmas every day. I can agree, however, that I certainly didn't always think this way.

When I was first born again and I was purely Christian and not at all dirtied by the world, I confess that I wanted to die and be with the father. The love was that strong. As time passes we realise that there is more to being a Christian than just wanting to be with the father. Isaiah 61 1:7 describes this:

The Spirit of the Sovereign LORD is on me,
because the LORD has anointed me
to proclaim good news to the poor.
He has sent me to bind up the broken-hearted,
to proclaim freedom for the captives
and release from darkness for the prisoners,
² to proclaim the year of the LORD's favour
and the day of vengeance of our God,
to comfort all who mourn,

3   *and provide for those who grieve in Zion—*
to bestow on them a crown of beauty
   instead of ashes,
the oil of joy
   instead of mourning,
and a garment of praise
   instead of a spirit of despair.
They will be called oaks of righteousness,
   a planting of the LORD
   for the display of his splendour.
      4 *They will rebuild the ancient ruins*
   and restore the places long devastated;
they will renew the ruined cities
   that have been devastated for generations.
5 *Strangers will shepherd your flocks;*
   foreigners will work your fields and vineyards.
6 *And you will be called priests of the LORD,*
   you will be named ministers of our God.
You will feed on the wealth of nations,
   and in their riches you will boast.
      7 *Instead of your shame*
   you will receive a double portion,
and instead of disgrace
   you will rejoice in your inheritance.
And so you will inherit a double portion in your land,
   and everlasting joy will be yours.

As you can see, we do have things to do on the earth for the father. We have a duty of care for the citizens of this world and it is also our duty to spread the word of the Lord and help others to come to faith or to accept God as their living Saviour. He is real, and it's the work of the devil that people are blinded to Him. They deny Him and worship other things or nothing at all. Atheism is fast growing and from the perspective of Christianity, it's hard to understand how someone can believe there's no God and creator of everything but when you are blinded, it's not your fault. I was blinded for a long time where I could not understand that a God could exist and even today, when I am busy with work or something else, I lose track of where I am with God. This is why it is important to make time for fellowship with God and for good works.

I struggled with "good works" for a long time. I still had the "get paid" mentality and I was sure that I could do good works and get paid for it and that would be the way forward. I think I had to rewire my mind in that "work" was for my survival and "good works" was for Him. I'm not altogether convinced that I've mastered it but when I do "good works", "work" seems to follow. I don't do "good works" so that "work" follows, it just seems to happen that way. I currently help out at a food bank. God knows I do this and sometimes I even get reminders. I might be tired or engaged in something when in my mind i hear "feed my people" which has to be a prompting. I do, however, think there's a mutual helping each other going on.

Very early in my Christian walk, I was thinking about starting a charity or business but I got the very definite impression that I should join in with something that already exists. You can do the same as there are many different charitable organisations. And you don't have to be fussy. If you are in the wrong place doing the wrong thing, then God will in some way make it clear to you that you shouldn't be there and that you should go somewhere else. This is one aspect of the opening and closing of doors that God is very good at. You might like to see it as a maze of life which contains many doors, which God opens and closes to provide you with your best tailored route to your very own destination. When you are following Gods directions, do not be disheartened when you hit a stumbling block or a closed door for this is all part of his plan. We stand up, we change direction and we continue.

As Christians, we should be walking in miracles and wonders and not just going to church on Sunday for our regular service. In the time of Jesus and the early church, this was normal or it became normal. It wasn't just Jesus who could make things happen. It wasn't just Jesus who could heal the sick. Peter did it. Paul did it. Everybody who has the holy spirit in them has the potential to heal the sick, cast out demons, raise the dead and speak in different tongues. This is what spirit filled is about. It is about not being a normal citizen but being a heavenly one, and there is a difference. I will be the first to admit that I don't fully use my gifting. I've laid hands on a few people in the past few years. That's not up to Jesus' standards by a long way. What I should be doing is going to the local hospital and putting the Doctors out of work!

So what does God say that, as Christians, we should be doing? In the old testament, there are many laws that the Jewish people must keep. There are pages of them, in fact, there are 613 of them. If it were law just to remember them, then most of us would fail.

These laws were the laws of the Jewish people and ranged from *1. To know that God exists* all the way to *613. To destroy the seed of Amalek (Amalek is a son of Esau's first-born son Eliphaz)*

But don't worry. The new testament arrived and in Galatians 5:18, we are told "But if ye be led of the Spirit, ye are not under the law. Well, that has to be good news for me. So we are not under the law, then what are we under? Simply put, we are under grace.

Grace can be seen as the big bonus about being a Christian. We mentioned that people sin and because of this sin we are then condemned, most probably to eternal damnation. The Up side is that as Christians we are free from the law and the law of sin, but don't forget, many of us have quite a few years left to live and are probably tempted by the devil, more often than not. Grace is Gods undeserved love and unmerited favour. I think that this is a really good way of putting it. Coupled with Grace is forgiveness.

Perhaps I do something I shouldn't. Maybe I took some money or let someone down. I then ask the father for genuine forgiveness in a simple prayer, something like "Father, please forgive me for acting the way I did, I shouldn't have done it and I repent". The Father then overlooks your sin and does not stack it against you in a big list of sins prepared for when you meet him. Remember, that when you eventually meet the father, it would be best to have a "Well done!" than a list to answer to. And besides which, since you are Christian, you don't want to displease the father even if he does love you, no matter what.

Of course, there is other grace. We say grace before a meal or we say The Grace prayer which is:

May the grace of our Lord Jesus Christ, and the love of God, and the fellowship of the Holy Spirit be with us all, now and evermore. Amen.

The way that we are looking at grace is that it is a nurturing mother or father who, when you fall, picks you up, brushes you off and put you back on track.

Every Christian is on a journey. The end result of this journey is holiness which in turn allows you into heaven. This is our goal, our destination and our joy. Believe me, there is nothing better than knowing that you will eventually be with the Father in the best place ever. We really are talking about a heaven or a place much better than what we could have experienced so far. You only have to look at encounters with heaven on the internet to get an idea. I have a friend who keeps having encounters of heaven and will tell me that he's been in the throne room or the library in heaven and although it can sound a little far-fetched, we have to remember that these things do exist. Heaven is a real place and as Christians, we are destined to be there. I had a tiny glimpse a few years ago when I was suddenly in a vision and I was nearly hit by a horse and on the horse was a princely man who might have fitted into a Robin Hood film but I couldn't understand why he didn't have a sword or a bow and arrows until I realised that this is Heaven and there is no need. There is no fighting or war or anything bad. The vision was very real. Visions are like dreams but they happen during the day when you are awake and afterwards, you feel a little unnerved for some time. This was all new to me because I hardly ever dream. Before I was saved I used to have nightmares rather than dreams and they were so bad, they were terrifying. So bad that either my brain stopped them or my memory erased them. Thank goodness that I'm now with God.

Since Heaven is so pure and perfect, there's no wonder that we take a long time to be prepared for it. If, as soon as you accepted Christ as your saviour, you were jettisoned up to heaven, I'm sure we would start altering this perfect state of heaven. There is an old saying of "If ever you find that perfect Church, don't join it because you'll spoil it" which may be appropriate for premature entry into heaven. Remember that Gods plan was to have a perfect world here until the beautiful Lucifer wanted the power of God for himself. God is recreating this perfect world and if you are Christian and the Lord is working on you, then you should rejoice. Truly it is an amazing thing to be on Gods list.

Now comes the age old question of "What if you're not Christian, does this mean that you can't get to heaven?". There is no true answer to that because nobody knows and understands God because our human brains are too limited to be able to think like God. But I do know that he came to us as Jesus and with a message that we have an eternal life waiting for us should we accept. He told Nicodemus in John 3 1-4.

3 Now there was a Pharisee, a man named Nicodemus who was a member of the Jewish ruling council. ² He came to Jesus at night and said, "Rabbi, we know that you are a teacher who has come from God. For no one could perform the signs you are doing if God were not with him." ³ Jesus replied, "Very truly I tell you, no one can see the kingdom of God unless they are born again.

As far as I know, only Christians can be born again. People of any faith can be "born again" but only the Christian faith contains people who are born again because you are Born again in Christ. Please bear in mind that faiths do not go to heaven. Individuals do. And, as a dear friend once said, "God is so amazing, he can do anything" which means don't be surprised who you might meet when you get to heaven. And don't judge. People can change and someone who you think wouldn't have a chance, may do in the next 10 or 20 years....... And beside which, no matter how much you study someone, follow them, ask others about them or anything else, you cannot see into their heart. God can and he does.

∞ ∞ ∞

CHAPTER 6   *Purchased at a price*

ho would you die for? For whom would you allow people to humiliate you, torture you and kill you? I'm sorry, but I'd really struggle to lose a finger for one of my friends. It's not that I don't love and care for them, it's just that I really wouldn't want to. But that's not the case for Jesus. He gave us all. And he did it out of love so that everybody in the world can get to know father God and have an escape route and a road to Heaven. We all know that Jesus could have commanded his armies of Angels to smite (old testament word!) the Romans and possibly the Jews but he didn't, he laid his life down for us. He didn't even put up a fight. He submitted his life, he gave it up for us. He could have done anything he wanted because he was God and he had the power of God. Instead he sacrificed himself so that we could live forever. It was more like suicide for the good of others.

Once we are in Christ, we have eternal life which means that we are no longer going to die at death but continue to live in Heaven. Thank goodness we don't have to go to hell. If you are not a saved Christian, then you probably do go to hell. Think of all the unsaved people in this world and then you'll start to understand why it was so important for the early disciples and those that followed, to spread the word or pass the message on that there is a future beyond death. In addition to that, we also have somewhere to stay. In the Bible, John tells us that Jesus says

"In my Father's house are many mansions: if it were not so, I would have told you. I go to prepare a place for you".

You might notice that two very significant names in the Bible are Adam and Jesus. In a way, Adam was the first Jesus because he was the father of all the people that ever lived. And Jesus was the father of all the people that have come to Christ and are born for the second time and of the spirit. You are a son of Adam until you are born again and then you are a son of God or Jesus (the same thing really).

In Christ, not only do you have you have eternal life but you also now have a different way to live. And this can be a difficult concept to bring into reality. In this world, you or your body has senses to tell you what is going on. In fact, you have five senses which are Touch, Sight, Taste, Smell and Sound. That's great, everything we need. But the bible changes things. The bible tells us not to depend on your senses. Your senses often start itching and need scratching. If you smoke, you crave cigarettes (as I once did). This is getting gratification from earthly things. Other examples might be porn or weed or coffee or chocolate. The body might tell you that you want drugs or sexual excitement but you need to change your command centre. By this, I mean that you need to be controlled not by your physical desires but now by your spiritual desires. As a born again Christian, you used to be of the flesh which means you used to have desires such as to smoke or look at porn of overeat or overdrink. Now that you are of Christ, you should now be controlled by spiritual things and the fleshy things that you used to do should be of the past. That's the idea anyway. You will probably find that you fail and you are annoyed with yourself. You are not alone. In Romans 7:19, Paul states that:

"For I do not the good I want to do, but the evil I do not want to do – this I keep on doing".

We might be talking about totally different things for you and I, but it does clearly show that Paul has a battle for righteousness which proves that it isn't easy, although it must be our aim. Paul is one of my heroes from the bible since he had a similar conversion to me and it is also a little comforting to know that he also had a struggle.

You will also find that you might do something you shouldn't and it wasn't that bad so you do it again. This repeats and repeats until you are some way away from God. You don't feel Him anymore and your mind is not on the Lord. It is, however, down to you to realise that you are separating from the spirit life and returning to the fleshy body life that you use to live in. Don't beat yourself up! This is exactly what the devil wants to happen to you. He wants to steal you away from God. He doesn't want you praising God for the good things in your life, he wants you caught up in things that take your mind and your heart away from God. The devil wants you worshipping him. And some people do. There are many cases in the world of people that worship satan or the devil. You are fortunate that you have found the Lord but your biggest effort might be ahead of you. You need to keep your faith and enthuse others with the love of God. You might prefer that the doors of heaven are flung open with fanfares playing and people cheering when you arrive rather than a sluggish entry.

Jesus effectively tells us to do good works or we are no good. In Mathew 5 he explains:

[13] *"You are the salt of the earth. But if the salt loses its saltiness, how can it be made salty again? It is no longer good for anything, except to be thrown out and trampled underfoot.*

52

[14] *"You are the light of the world. A town built on a hill cannot be hidden.* [15] *Neither do people light a lamp and put it under a bowl. Instead they put it on its stand, and it gives light to everyone in the house.* [16] *In the same way, let your light shine before others, that they may see your good deeds and glorify your Father in heaven.*

As a Christian you should be standing tall for God. That lamp on the table should be you doing good works in society for all to see and they should then understand that you are doing these for God. Paul writes a letter to the Galatians, a group of early churches in Galatia.

Let us not lose heart in doing good, for in due time we will reap if we do not grow weary. So then, while we have opportunity, let us do good to all people, and especially to those who are of the household of the faith.

Paul clearly understands the principle of doing good works. I have found that good works are often for little or no money and the recipients are not always the most thankful. In these cases, to save yourself from desperation, I often adjust my mind and realise that I am doing these good works for God. I have also worked with homeless people and at times I justify the tiredness by thinking that if my daughter became homeless after I've died, I sure hope that someone like me, helps her.

Also remember that we are all created by God. But not all have turned to and accepted Christ as their Lord and Saviour but we all could. Once you do this, Gods love is not based on your actions, it is based on you having the spirit of the living lord within you. In Romans 6, Paul discussed whether we can still sin.

What shall we say, then? Shall we go on sinning so that grace may increase? [2] *By no means! We are those who have died to sin; how can we live in it any longer?* [3] *Or don't you know that all of us who were baptized into Christ Jesus were baptized into his death?* [4] *We were therefore buried with him through baptism into death in order that, just as Christ was raised from the dead through the glory of the Father, we too may live a new life.*

⁵ For if we have been united with him in a death like his, we will certainly also be united with him in a resurrection like his. ⁶ For we know that our old self was crucified with him so that the body ruled by sin might be done away with, that we should no longer be slaves to sin— ⁷ because anyone who has died has been set free from sin.

I think that I can still sin. I could, if I wanted, repeat some things from my previous life but the longer that I am in Christ, the less I want to. I think the key to what Paul is saying is the slavery to sin. When I was a smoker, I was a slave to the cigarette. They had me craving them for a long number of years. Soon after I was born again, I was set free from the addiction and I no longer smoke. The addiction made me a slave but because I am in Christ, I am no longer a slave to ungodly things. You can probably think of more sinful examples but I assure you, so can I.

In 1 John, he too indicates that sin is now undesired in a godly person.

"Everyone who sins breaks the law; in fact, sin is lawlessness. ⁵ But you know that he appeared so that he might take away our sins. And in him is no sin. ⁶ No one who lives in him keeps on sinning. No one who continues to sin has either seen him or known him."

If you choose to practice sin you will soon harden your heart until you are so far away from God that you cannot communicate with Him. That is a place you don't want to be in. Every time you hear about people dying on the news, you should be upset. Generally, we are not but we should be. People have got hardened hearts and this is one way of knowing. *Yes, but not specific to the 10 command*

Jesus told us that if you break one of the 10 Commandments then you have broken the lot. Similarly, in God's eyes, every sin is the same. This leaves us with no excuses such as "oh it's just a little sin" or "it doesn't matter, it's just a white lie". You can't change or bend the rules to suit you. This is God's game and we play by his rules or not at all.

I just thought I'd also mention about relationship and marriage. A common problem is the marriage of partners outside the people of God. If you are in Christ, you need to find a partner who is the same. If you were to marry a non-Christian, you may be setting yourself up for trouble. You are a child of God. It makes no sense to be with a child of the devil. It is recommended that you marry within the faith. It is also wise to let God be your matchmaker and this you do through prayer.

You were purchased at a price. Ephesians 1 tells us that we were chosen.

¹¹ In him we were also chosen, having been predestined according to the plan of him who works out everything in conformity with the purpose of his will, ¹² in order that we, who were the first to put our hope in Christ, might be for the praise of his glory. ¹³ And you also were included in Christ when you heard the message of truth, the gospel of your salvation. When you believed, you were marked in him with a seal, the promised Holy Spirit, ¹⁴ who is a deposit guaranteeing our inheritance until the redemption of those who are God's possession—to the praise of his glory.

Here we find that we were marked with the seal. A seal is permanent and will not rub off or drop off. You have been chosen and sealed and the Holy Spirit is always with you. You are a done deal. You just have to learn how to walk in your new Christian shoes. It's hard not to feel special since you've been chosen and Jesus has died for you so that you can have eternal life. You should have firm foundation being rooted in the knowledge that God loves you, regardless of anything that you did in the past. We all have an end date. The difference is that we, as Christians, can even look forward to ours.

contradict yourself

∞ ∞ ∞

CHAPTER 7   *Prayer*

*T*he Lords' prayer, to me, was something you say at school or at Church and it just means that you are Christian. The Lord's prayer, many years later, means much more than that and I'll tell you why. In Matthew 6:9-13 Jesus tell us:

⁹ *"This, then, is how you should pray:*

"'Our Father in heaven,
hallowed be your name,
¹⁰ *your kingdom come,*
your will be done,
   on earth as it is in heaven.
¹¹ *Give us today our daily bread.*
¹² *And forgive us our debts,*
   as we also have forgiven our debtors.
¹³ *And lead us not into temptation,*
   but deliver us from the evil one.'

As a child, who has never spoke to their parents? Perhaps orphans or people who were ostracised or people who were adopted. This is not a problem because in Psalm 68, God is described as the father of the Fatherless (and also in a beautiful song by Jason Upton). I know a few people who are fatherless and who have been born again. I also find it interesting that I was saved just after my dad had died. A Psalm reads:

Sing to God, sing in praise of his name,
extol him who rides on the clouds;
rejoice before him—his name is the LORD.
[5] *A father to the fatherless, a defender of widows,*
is God in his holy dwelling.
[6] *God sets the lonely in families,*
he leads out the prisoners with singing;
but the rebellious live in a sun-scorched land.

God is now my Father but I share him, so he's Our Father and he's in Heaven, just like the Lord's prayer. Heaven is a genuine and real place and that's where my father is. How awesome is that. Heaven is where all our fathers are in One. I've said before that the moment I was born again, I strangely had one desire. I wanted to die and to be with father God. All I wanted was to be home with father God. Years later I know why I wasn't immediately evacuated but I do now live a better life knowing that I'm Christian, knowing where my father is and where my final destination is (and not just Chapter 12).

A simple example would be if you were 8 years old and lived in a house in London with your mum and dad and your dad had to go and work full time in Sweden. You might send him pictures, letters, emails and you would definitely call him on the telephone even just to say "hi" or that you love him. Well, here I am in England and my father is in Heaven. The only way of talking to my father is through Prayer and I might start with "Our Father, who art in Heaven". You might say that he is not exclusively in Heaven be because he is here with us. I have no doubt that he is watching over me as I write this book. There are complexities in Christianity and one of them is that Our Father is in Heaven and he is also here with us. That being said, we are also coexisting with him. It also tells us that Heaven can also be here with us, just like God.

Don't think of God as anything other than a living being. You should talk to him as often as you can. I always start my day by saying the Lord's Prayer and finish my day by saying the Lord's Prayer. I can see it as picking up the phone in the morning and putting it down at night.

The Lord's prayer is the prayer that Jesus himself taught us. In doing this alone, he's telling us to communicate with the Father. Quite often in the Bible, Jesus himself went off to pray. And that's another confusing thing because we might ask why he, as God, is praying to himself. I think the answer comes under the mysteries of God or perhaps as a tri part being, each of the Father, the Son and the Holy spirit need to communicate. I was recently talking to a Christadelphian who are a type of Christianity who believe that the trinity are, in fact, separate. I can understand that too. For me, the Trinity is the hardest part of Christianity to fully understand so I always resort to the Venn diagram of three interlinking circles. I find that this helps.

I've heard it asked why we pray for bread every day, even when we have some. Just to clarify, I believe that the bread talked about in this prayer is the bread of life, the bread that we need to exist. This is not a loaf of Hovis but a catch-all for what keeps us alive and spiritually alive more than anything else. That's my understanding.

The longer I lived as a Christian, the more my prayers developed and grew. I still always keep the Lord's prayer but have learnt to expand on this. There's a massive part missing from a lot of people's prayers, or the prayers that I've heard and that is thanks giving. I am so grateful for what God has done for me that I have to repeatedly thank him for saving me. I thank him for my parents, I thanks him for my daughter, I thank him for my house, my sisters, my brothers and the list goes on. You can thank him for the sun in the sky and the water from your tap. Remember, God created everything and you can be thankful for an awful lot. I like to think that the "thanks" puts God in a good mood as it would please me if someone kept thanking me.

These are the prayers that I often pray. This shows you the sort of thing that I do but I am not saying you have to pray these prayers. Pray what is suitable for you. You can get prayers from all different places including the internet and prayer books.

I give thanks to the Lord, for his mercy and living kindness that endures forever. I am not superior to anyone else. All my gifts and abilities are from God, and not anything that I have is apart from him. God alone is judge of all things. Amen.

I am redeemed from sin, guilt and condemnation. I am redeemed from anger, bitterness, jealousy, fear and I am free to love God, love myself and love other people. Amen.

In God I trust; I shall not be afraid. What can flesh do to me? I declare that I have already defeated the agents of the anti-Christ as he that is in me is greater that he that is in the world. Amen.

I come to you today to obtain grace to help in my time of need. You know all the things I am facing and I thank you that I can be strengthened inwardly by your grace. Thank you for your strength and ability to do all that is set before me. I ask you to load me up with extra grace and spiritual blessing. Today, I declare, I am strong in the Lord and the power of his grace. Amen.

I release my spirit into the natural and I command the Holy Ghost that I walk with Unction, Promptings and Direction. I ask you to loose your angels to remove any demonic influence in my life right now, I bind my tongue to be a holy tongue. I pray for the spirit of wisdom and revelation to dream in the spirit world. Amen.

I bind the spirit of witchcraft. I plead the blood against it. I declare it under my feet and cancel the assignments. In Jesus's name, Amen.

I declare I release prosperity will be my portion, blessing will follow me and the Lord will redeem my past and transform my future in Jesus's name, Amen.

When you are born again and spirit led, you may become attracted to the Pentecostal movement and you may like to reside here. Here they do a lot of decreeing and declaring which is similar to stating but with the backing of God. When you say something with the backing of God, you now have the authority of Jesus when you say something. It is just as if Jesus said those words himself. You can therefore expect things to happen.

Sometimes things don't change and that's when you have to look at your own faith. You command something to happen and it doesn't materialise. Do you have disbelief? Do you 100% believe that it will happen. When Jesus says you need to come to the Father as a child, he may mean that you have to have to mind of a child and have the belief of a child which is often very unswerving and unaffected by the many things around us in life.

Notice also that in one of my prayers, I bind my tongue. It is often too easy to say the wrong thing by mistake and this usually happens when you are in good company. By binding my tongue, I am stopping it spurt out wrong and undesired words. God doesn't want us speaking foul language and I used to, a lot. This will help me keep face. And as a Christian it is important that I do and that I do not slip back into old ways.

I will say that my main problem as a new or maturing Christian is that I get busy or lazy. Either way, I can forget to pray. When I don't pray, nothing bad happens but nothing particularly good does either. The longer it goes on the more distant I become from God. I've heard it described as having a fire burning inside of you and you stoke it up every day but when you forget, the fire dims until it is almost extinguished. The importance of regular prayer is paramount to a Christian. If you're not praying regularly, you have to do a self-assessment. As a Christian, you should want to pray and talk to the father and if you don't, there may be some blockage which usually comes from the devil.

It is quite beneficial if you can pray with a clear mind. All too often when we look for silence and peace, there are things buzzing around in our heads such as things people have said or what you are going to buy next or your latest worry. It is like magic but you can control your mind when you have the keys. You control access to your mind by controlling what goes in and what stays in. It is your mind so you need to protect it. Keeping the peace often entails getting rid of junk. If someone has said that you are no good, it will resonate inside your mind. "I reject that statement, in the name of Jesus" will clear that thought away and many others like that, but I find you have to reject the thoughts individually like a filtering system. Only allow good thoughts to muster in your head. And guess what, you'll be a much more positive person.

There will be times when you will have worries. We all have worries from time to time. You are with God now and part of that is the ability to pass on our worries. For example, if you are worrying about how to pay the rent, the ordinary person would keep on worrying until a solution is found. The Christian might pray "Lord Father, I am really worried about paying the rent because you know my financial situation. Lord I give you this problem and I pray that you can help." The Christian then passes the problem to God and carries on without worrying. Intervention is on its way in some shape or form. And it's never early. God is our provider and he does provide but he's never early but fortunately he's never late either. He is always bang on just when you need him. When he decides

There are many books about praying and how to pray but I suggest that you pray from your heart. Try to always pray with thanksgiving and try to recognise who he is by calling him almighty God, wonderful God, amazing God etcetera. He likes this and it is worth repeating because I think it is really important. Some people just give him a list of things that they want but it is much better to talk to him. More often than not you will find yourself talking to a silent one, but he is listening. He loves you and He loves to hear your voice and He loves to hear you pray. I've also heard it said that God so loves to hear your voice that you better be careful when you don't pray because things might go wrong so that you do turn to prayer.

Most marriages that fail do so because of poor communication. You have a marriage with God and you must ensure that you are communicating well. Regular prayer is a must and so is meaningful prayer. Before you pray, you may even write down the people you know that need healing prayer, help or any other kind of assistance. Praying for other people is pleasing to God.

A point that I should mention is that it is fine to pray for yourself. Some people think that it is not right or that they are not worthy but you are a child of God and no one has more right to ask of your father than you. Be careful what you ask for because God will not feed a greedy gut. He will provide for your welfare and for the advancement of his kingdom.

The reply to your prayer is also varied. Sometimes I have prayed and things happen almost instantly. Once I had stayed in a gym way too late for my daytime membership and I was worried about getting out without being spotted. Just after I had prayed about this, the fire alarm went off. Bingo! On other occasions, you can pray about something and nothing happens. Days and weeks pass and you realise that you are probably not going to see the end result. The important lesson to learn is that you do not control God. You can only ask and God decides what he actions and when. Remember that when you became Christian, you effectively entered into a brand new world and world with different rules and different ways of doing things. You might imagine that you have accepted gameplay in Gods world and now you have to play by his rules and you will discover that he is very rarely in a hurry. The reason for this is that you are operating in a world that is a world of clocks whereas God operates out of time - no clocks. The good news is that he is watching you.

No one wants to pray

You might have seen people praying with their hands outstretched or their palms turned facing upwards. It's a common thing and I have seen it in both the Church of England and the Pentecostal movement. I believe/your hands act similar to satellites in that the glory of God can be received and transmitted through the palms of the hands. If you are in the presence of God, you will want to open your hands and possibly raise your arms to receive His glory which is a wonderful thing. It feels tingly at times.

There are other reactions to being in the glory of God. One man I knew used to shiver quite violently. My hands shake and sometimes my whole arm and that's the same for a good friend of mine. I once witnessed a man's whole body shaking and that was a sight. With regards to my hands shaking, I can force it to stop but it is much better to side with God and let his glory work though you than to be swayed by onlookers who may find it embarrassing. That's their problem. You are with God and your eternal life is with God. That is what is important.

I'm not going to say a trick, but a key to making prayer work in *Re word* your favour is often influencing your providers. On a few occasions I have required more work than I had. I currently work through teaching agencies who organise and provide work in schools for me and it is logical to pray that I receive more work from them. I haven't yet seen any positive results from this. I tried to pray for my wealth to increase as a result of more work but this yields no results either. I even tried praying that the schools would have particular shortages and therefore I would be required. That didn't work either but what did work is this. I prayed that the agency staff could be the best and most effective agency staff, working to the best of their ability. Indirectly, I had ordered myself some work.

Needs finishing statement

∞ ∞ ∞

CHAPTER 8   *Treasures in Heaven*

*Y*ou are always being watched. In England there are cameras everywhere. They are in shops, they are on the motorways and they are in parking lots. You can watch detective programs and they can access street cameras to find out what people were doing prior to a crime; they can even remotely access your mobile phone records. Your personal details are on a computer somewhere. The organisation you work for logs your personal information, so does the electricity company that you use, the water company etc. I recently lost my passport along with a few other things. Soon after I had realised what had happened, I felt God speak this verse of Mathew 6. It helped me relax a little and focused my mind on what really matters and it brought me into complete agreement as I was sure that the bag had been stolen.

[19] *"Do not store up for yourselves treasures on earth, where moths and vermin destroy, and where thieves break in and steal.* [20] *But store up for yourselves treasures in heaven, where moths and vermin do not destroy, and where thieves do not break in and steal.* [21] *For where your treasure is, there your heart will be also.*

It also made me think that I should really be doing more for the kingdom of God. Have I stored enough in Heaven? Well, probably not. I do some work in the compassionate ministries but I could always do more. For a long time after I was born again I had dreams of building charity organisations or creating websites for Christians but never actually did anything. Then I started seeing charity flyers and got the message that I didn't have to start something afresh, I could join in to something that already existed. This I really did need to do because as James 2 14:26 tells us:

14 What good is it, my brothers and sisters, if someone claims to have faith but has no deeds? Can such faith save them? 15 Suppose a brother or a sister is without clothes and daily food. 16 If one of you says to them, "Go in peace; keep warm and well fed," but does nothing about their physical needs, what good is it? 17 In the same way, faith by itself, if it is not accompanied by action, is dead.

18 But someone will say, "You have faith; I have deeds."
Show me your faith without deeds, and I will show you my faith by my deeds. 19 You believe that there is one God. Good! Even the demons believe that and shudder.
20 You foolish person, do you want evidence that faith without deeds is useless? 21 Was not our father Abraham considered righteous for what he did when he offered his son Isaac on the altar? 22 You see that his faith and his actions were working together, and his faith was made complete by what he did. 23 And the scripture was fulfilled that says, "Abraham believed God, and it was credited to him as righteousness," and he was called God's friend. 24 You see that a person is considered righteous by what they do and not by faith alone.

25 In the same way, was not even Rahab the prostitute considered righteous for what she did when she gave lodging to the spies and sent them off in a different direction? 26 As the body without the spirit is dead, so faith without deeds is dead.

There is always room to do more good works. Good works is looking after others. People that are less fortunate than yourself. I always fancied going abroad to do mission work and perhaps one day I will, but at the moment I'm helping out on home shores.

Interestingly, there was a case of an old lady that was far too old to be any practical use serving the Lord, especially since her eyes were failing. But she was of use because she could pray for people and that's what she did and that gave her a sense of purpose too. If you are lost about how to do good works, you can always start by praying for others.

I find that God seldom gives you what you want but is more likely to give you opportunity. If I am desperate for a new job, I am more likely to come across jobs to apply for than having someone knock on my door with a contract to sign. He is for you and works with you but you have to also do some work yourself. The important thing to remember is not to stop praying. Pray for opportunities to do good works if you're looking for them and can't immediately see any. You will be surprised how much is going on behind the scenes.

I once read a Facebook post about a lady who had some very nice dresses that were saved for a special occasion. When she died, the husband found them in the wardrobe and was extremely upset that she hadn't had the chance to wear them. Now is your opportunity not to save up things for your earthly future but to invest in your eternal future which is far more important. Of course you can have possessions and you can have superfluous possessions but be sure that you will die. Let's make sure we have more provision where we are going rather than where we have been. And this is done through good works. Be inspired to help others.

I have great admiration for people who have given their whole life to Gods good works. Mother Theresa springs to mind but there are plenty others. God is not completely preoccupied with good works in the shape of mission. There are a lot of other things that he values too. He is a God of life and not just a God of the poor and unfortunate. I recall a single father I met on a course, searching his mind for what good he can do in society for God. I asked him how many children he has and it was a few. I told him that his good works was probably bringing up those children. He hadn't thought of that.

I know in the past I have had the sense that God is pleased with me and I have also been told that by sisters in the faith. This is when I think, how can he be pleased with me when I don't even think I'm up to scratch and I'm sure that his standards will be way higher than mine. After all, he is looking for perfect human beings to take to heaven. How can he be happy with me when, from time to time, I'm still dipping in an out of my old traits? The important answer to this is that when I was born again, my old spirit died and a new spirit was put inside of me. Back again to Nicodemus. So God can look at me and there is perfection in me. It is in my spirit and slowly, very slowly this perfect spirit man is dissipating or spreading into me. I can tell you honestly that it is a gradual process with hiccups, but I am so glad that God never starts something and does not finish it. If you are reading this book, then he's probably working on you too which has to be good news. And the more time I spend in worship and in biblical texts, the quicker I would expect this process to be. Jesus is my role model and I want to be like him. Look at the character of Jesus and become like him. This is our goal and what a worthy goal it is. And what did Jesus do a lot? He prayed.

Mark 1:35 tells us that Jesus prayed.
*"Very early in the morning, while it was still dark, **Jesus** got up, left the house and went off to a solitary place, where he **prayed**".*
Luke 5:16 tells us that Jesus prayed.

*"**Jesus** often withdrew to lonely places and **prayed**".*

John 17:1 tells us that Jesus prayed.

*"After **Jesus** said this, he looked toward heaven and **prayed**: "Father, the hour has come. Glorify your Son, that your Son may glorify you""*.

If Jesus prayed, then so should we. You have been born again into the spirit world and now you are pretty much the same as Jesus. You have access to Father God just the same as Jesus did but we don't seem to use it the same as he did. This is the big shame about Christianity in that a lot of born again Christians don't actually realise who they are. They don't realise that they are sons and daughters of the almighty God and that His power is available to them just like it was for Jesus. This may be largely down to the devil scheming to take power away from us and make us feel as if we are just normal or even sub-normal. There are even times when I question myself whether I really am Christian. In times like these, I am fortunate that I can speak in tongues and then ask myself when I learnt to do that. The answer is that I didn't and it is supernatural and therefore, yes, there you have a little proof to myself that there is a God. As daft as it might sound, probably the main reason I needed the gift of tongues was for this.

During your walk with Jesus, you will most likely experience crisis. This will come in all shapes and forms but do not loose heart. As we know, the year is already divided up into seasons and after one season is the next. Similarly, your crisis will last, not forever, but for a season. Ecclesiastes explains the use of "season" clearly.

*"There is a time for everything, and a **season** for every activity under the heavens: a time to be born and a time to die, a time to plant and a time to uproot, a time to kill and a time to heal, a time to tear down and a time to build, ..."*

But be warned, God can use a season to shape you and to make you into a stronger, more robust character. This means that he might bring you challenges and obstacles which may not be the comfortable route that you might wish for. You will be surprised what God can do and what he does for your benefit and for the benefit of His kingdom. Whilst Paul was writing letters in a Roman prison thousands of years ago, he didn't know that he was writing seven books of the Bible.

∞ ∞ ∞

CHAPTER 9   *Dreaming, Healing and Miracles*

I received the gift of tongues approximately two years after I had been saved. I had always wanted to speak another language and even after working for an international organisation in London, I still couldn't learn one particular language due to constantly changing the country that I was talking to and the different nationalities of the people sitting next to me. That may have influenced my desire for tongues or because it was the Fathers language that I could talk to him with or maybe because I once had it on the very first morning after conversion but it was taken from me because I just wanted to show off and call my friends. Either way, I desperately wanted tongues. Two years after coming to faith, I remember saying to God that "more than anything else, I wanted to speak in tongues!" and I meant it. Soon after, I was praying in another language and have ever since. It's not that I'm super special that I got what I asked for, this was because I had a desperation, an unshakeable desire for the gift of Tongues. Subsequent research tells me that when I speak in tongues, I am speaking in Ancient Hebrew, the language of God's chosen people from the Old Testament. An expert in Hebrew told me this. If that's not a miracle, then I don't know what is. You may have had a similar experience and I really enjoy listening to other people's experiences. It took two years and a lot of determination for me to speak in tongues so if you don't have the gift, then my advice is to decide if it is something that you want to get desperate for and don't give up and don't stop asking. Jesus did tell us in the bible to ask and we shall receive and with Tongues, this is what happened albeit that I asked out of desperation. Interestingly, if you want to know what you are saying when you are speaking in tongues, pray to the Father for interpretation of your tongues. I have done this and I received an instant translation.

I also believe that God does determine which spiritual gifts we receive and when. Some believe that all our spiritual gifts are received when we come to Christ but I would argue that that is not the case. So too would Paul in Corinthians who tells us we should strive after gifts which clearly indicates that they are freely available to us but not handed on mass.

Some people believe that all gifts, healings and miracles are only applicable to the time of Jesus. This is not the case. They are still happening today and I know this for sure. Following a road traffic accident when I was sixteen, I had a broken right leg and a thrombosis in the left. This resulted in a pretty much trouser covered life since I was left with one thin leg and one reddish swollen left leg. The specialist surgeon at the hospital advised that no one should ever operate on my left swollen leg because the main artery was blocked and the leg was literally surviving using secondary veins. He told me that I would surely lose my leg. Many years later, my vicar laid hands on my legs because one was slightly shorter than the other and this gave me back pain from time to time. Nothing really happened. When I returned home, I was a little disappointed so I headed to bed. As I did, a big pain grabbed my left leg near my knee. I am thinking that I need to call emergency services, the ambulance or something drastic. What happened was incredible because I believe that veins were being unblocked or were enlarging to massively reduced the swelling on the left ankle. There is still a difference in my legs but I now feel that I now have two very similar legs rather than a fat one and a thin one. This was amazing. God does what no doctor can. There are plenty of other testimonies about healing, you just have to look for them.

I went on a faith course at the local Cathedral and I sat on a table with a very pleasant girl who told how she had been abroad with missionaries and had witnessed people receiving their sight and the lame walking. It was just what I needed to hear. Hebrews 13:8 tells us that Jesus is always the same.

"Jesus Christ is the same yesterday and today and forever".

It is right. Jesus is not physically here as he was in biblical times, but he is here through Christians. We have the power of Jesus and we should be able to do everything that Jesus could do. I like to think of it as if we are Gods fingers. Jesus, the man is no longer here on earth but God has us. We are like His Jesus.

Since I've been born again I've come to realise that there is no luck. I used to think of things being lucky or similarly things being unlucky. As a Christian you no longer have luck but you have "from God". I've noticed a lot things have happened "from God" and I've made a list of them. Some of these are what you might call mini miracles or things that happen in your favour which seem a little strange. I once let a non-Christian friend view my list of miracles and I soon wished I hadn't. He was fairly well convinced that I was perhaps mentally unstable. But since you're reading this, you may have also had small miracles happen in your life that are difficult to explain to non-believers. What I suggest you do is to write down all these little favorable moments in a list somewhere. One day you may look back and then things might make more sense. I was told to keep a list of them because they might indicate where I was going on my journey with Christ. This is not the case yet, but I certainly have it in mind.

Miracles do happen. Another instance is where a Church leader at the Pentecostal church I was attending stood up and said "You might have noticed that I am no longer wearing glasses". He has indeed been healed. Another Church minister or prophet that I know was cured of dyslexia and described how great it was to be able to buy and read the most complex book he could find and was proud of it. Amazing to find that miracles and healings are for today. They're not lodged in the past but are active and present today.

What I also find miraculous is the dreams and visions that we have. I think some are general and some are messages from God. I spent most of my life not dreaming. When I did dream they weren't really dreams, they were horrible nightmares which left me scared to the core. Probably as a protection, my mind stopped remembering them. It wasn't until after I had been saved or born again that I started dreaming. One of these very first dreams was in a world war two scenario where I was on the run from the enemy and a family rushed me into the back of a truck and took me to a safe house or barn in France, saying that "You're with us now". I took this to mean that these were the Christians and I had been saved from the enemy. I had another dream some years later, where I was on a post-war train saying goodbye to a woman and remaining with a man in a raincoat and a Trilby hat. A good while later the lady vicar left our local Church and was replace by a man vicar. It wasn't until I read back through my notes that I realised the significance of this dream. I believe that these two are examples of God dreams. God dreams are the message dreams that come from God. We have plenty of dreams that are not so important and as such we tend not to remember them. If they are dreams from God, we remember them and with quite good clarity. That's how we can tell.

Dreaming is not something that is made up. We all do it and it is all tied into the way that our brains work and process information.

As Christians, this is a way that we can be communicated with by our God and a method that he uses and it's not new.

Prophecy is a prediction of what will happen in the future. Prophecy came to some prominent people in the bible through dreams and will continue to do so in new testament times. Just because Joseph and Daniel the dreamer lived in old testament times doesn't mean that you and me can't hear from God through dreams and visions. If you are not and you would like to, I suggest that you tell God that you desire to and set your heart on hearing from Him. Here is an example of Daniel interpreting a dream of Nebuchadnezzar.

2 *In the second year of his reign, Nebuchadnezzar had dreams; his mind was troubled and he could not sleep. ² So the king summoned the magicians, enchanters, sorcerers and astrologers to tell him what he had dreamed. When they came in and stood before the king, ³ he said to them, "I have had a dream that troubles me and I want to know what it means.[b]"*

⁴ Then the astrologers answered the king, "May the king live forever! Tell your servants the dream, and we will interpret it."

⁵ The king replied to the astrologers, "This is what I have firmly decided: If you do not tell me what my dream was and interpret it, I will have you cut into pieces and your houses turned into piles of rubble. ⁶ But if you tell me the dream and explain it, you will receive from me gifts and rewards and great honour. So tell me the dream and interpret it for me."

⁷ Once more they replied, "Let the king tell his servants the dream, and we will interpret it."

⁸ Then the king answered, "I am certain that you are trying to gain time, because you realize that this is what I have firmly decided: ⁹ If you do not tell me the dream, there is only one penalty for you. You have conspired to tell me misleading and wicked things, hoping the situation will change. So then, tell me the dream, and I will know that you can interpret it for me."

¹⁰ *The astrologers answered the king, "There is no one on earth who can do what the king asks! No king, however great and mighty, has ever asked such a thing of any magician or enchanter or astrologer. ¹¹ What the king asks is too difficult. No one can reveal it to the king except the gods, and they do not live among humans."*

¹² *This made the king so angry and furious that he ordered the execution of all the wise men of Babylon. ¹³ So the decree was issued to put the wise men to death, and men were sent to look for Daniel and his friends to put them to death.*

¹⁴ *When Arioch, the commander of the king's guard, had gone out to put to death the wise men of Babylon, Daniel spoke to him with wisdom and tact. ¹⁵ He asked the king's officer, "Why did the king issue such a harsh decree?" Arioch then explained the matter to Daniel. ¹⁶ At this, Daniel went in to the king and asked for time, so that he might interpret the dream for him.*

¹⁷ *Then Daniel returned to his house and explained the matter to his friends Hananiah, Mishael and Azariah. ¹⁸ He urged them to plead for mercy from the God of heaven concerning this mystery, so that he and his friends might not be executed with the rest of the wise men of Babylon. ¹⁹ During the night the mystery was revealed to Daniel in a vision. Then Daniel praised the God of heaven ²⁰ and said:*

> *"Praise be to the name of God for ever and ever;*
> *wisdom and power are his.*

²¹ *He changes times and seasons;*
> *he deposes kings and raises up others.*
He gives wisdom to the wise
> *and knowledge to the discerning.*

²² *He reveals deep and hidden things;*
> *he knows what lies in darkness,*
> *and light dwells with him.*

²³ *I thank and praise you, God of my ancestors:*
> *You have given me wisdom and power,*

you have made known to me what we asked of you,
  you have made known to us the dream of the king."

  Daniel then Interprets the Dream:
²⁴ *Then Daniel went to Arioch, whom the king had appointed to execute the wise men of Babylon, and said to him, "Do not execute the wise men of Babylon. Take me to the king, and I will interpret his dream for him."*

²⁵ *Arioch took Daniel to the king at once and said, "I have found a man among the exiles from Judah who can tell the king what his dream means."*

²⁶ *The king asked Daniel (also called Belteshazzar), "Are you able to tell me what I saw in my dream and interpret it?"*

²⁷ *Daniel replied, "No wise man, enchanter, magician or diviner can explain to the king the mystery he has asked about, ²⁸ but there is a God in heaven who reveals mysteries. He has shown King Nebuchadnezzar what will happen in days to come. Your dream and the visions that passed through your mind as you were lying in bed are these:*

²⁹ *"As Your Majesty was lying there, your mind turned to things to come, and the revealer of mysteries showed you what is going to happen. ³⁰ As for me, this mystery has been revealed to me, not because I have greater wisdom than anyone else alive, but so that Your Majesty may know the interpretation and that you may understand what went through your mind.*

³¹ *"Your Majesty looked, and there before you stood a large statue—an enormous, dazzling statue, awesome in appearance. ³² The head of the statue was made of pure gold, its chest and arms of silver, its belly and thighs of bronze, ³³ its legs of iron, its feet partly of iron and partly of baked clay. ³⁴ While you were watching, a rock was cut out, but not by human hands. It struck the statue on its feet of iron and clay and smashed them. ³⁵ Then the iron, the clay, the bronze, the silver and the gold were all broken to pieces and became like chaff on a threshing floor in the summer. The wind swept them away without leaving a trace. But the rock that struck the statue became a huge mountain and filled the whole earth.*

[36] "This was the dream, and now we will interpret it to the king. [37] Your Majesty, you are the king of kings. The God of heaven has given you dominion and power and might and glory; [38] in your hands he has placed all mankind and the beasts of the field and the birds in the sky. Wherever they live, he has made you ruler over them all. You are that head of gold.

[39] "After you, another kingdom will arise, inferior to yours. Next, a third kingdom, one of bronze, will rule over the whole earth. [40] Finally, there will be a fourth kingdom, strong as iron—for iron breaks and smashes everything—and as iron breaks things to pieces, so it will crush and break all the others. [41] Just as you saw that the feet and toes were partly of baked clay and partly of iron, so this will be a divided kingdom; yet it will have some of the strength of iron in it, even as you saw iron mixed with clay. [42] As the toes were partly iron and partly clay, so this kingdom will be partly strong and partly brittle. [43] And just as you saw the iron mixed with baked clay, so the people will be a mixture and will not remain united, any more than iron mixes with clay.

[44] "In the time of those kings, the God of heaven will set up a kingdom that will never be destroyed, nor will it be left to another people. It will crush all those kingdoms and bring them to an end, but it will itself endure forever. [45] This is the meaning of the vision of the rock cut out of a mountain, but not by human hands—a rock that broke the iron, the bronze, the clay, the silver and the gold to pieces.

"The great God has shown the king what will take place in the future. The dream is true and its interpretation is trustworthy."

[46] Then King Nebuchadnezzar fell prostrate before Daniel and paid him honour and ordered that an offering and incense be presented to him. [47] The king said to Daniel, "Surely your God is the God of gods and the Lord of kings and a revealer of mysteries, for you were able to reveal this mystery."

This is just one example where dreams/visions are really important and are messages from God. Notice that Nebuchadnezzar first summoned *magicians, enchanters, sorcerers and astrologers.* These people are not of God and therefore could not interpret the dream that was from God. It takes Gods people to understand God given dreams and visions.

Prior to being born again, I had no interest in reading the Bible and no ability to do so. It made no or little sense. I couldn't stand reading it. I made my mind up to read the bible when I was younger but just couldn't. Now that I am from God, you can't stop me reading the bible and associated books. Some might say that I'm "in the zone" but really, I'm in Christ and I now have my eyes opened to the truth. Daniel had his eyes open to the truth and the magicians, enchanter's sorcerers and astrologers were all false. They couldn't interpret Gods word so why should we ever listen to them? Even to this day, I even refuse to read my horoscope. When I lived and worked in London, I used to love reading the horoscope whilst on the tube on my way to work. Today, I try and live by Gods direction and no one else's. I refer to them as "horror scopes" which are likely to give me either false hope or take me down paths that are unintended.

Once you are with God, you have to do what every child of His should do, and that is to pursue him, love him and as we mentioned earlier, talk to him though prayer. I wouldn't even bother with anything else.

Since I have been with God, I have also noticed that He can speak to us through nature. It might sound mad but on more than one occasion I have had a white bird fly in front of my car. I believe that this was for no other purpose than to let me know that He is still with me. What I am saying here though, is not to expect the normal but to rejoice in your harmony with nature, after all, He created all things, did he not?

The important point to gather from this chapter and I'm probably repeating myself, is that all Dreaming, Healing and Miracles are for today. As a Christian, these are the things that I believe you should be walking in and if you are not, you have to question why. Don't forget that the devil or satan are constantly working against us which is why they are referred to as the Anti-Christ. This is perhaps why you at times feel distant from God but you are far from lost. Since you are with Christ you are found anyway. It has happened to me and the word from God is to "press in" or get more involved with him or become more interested in him. In times like these I have even forced myself to read my Bible just to get started. You can even pray to the Father to know Him better or to have a better relationship with Him.

The New Testament tells us of the many miracles of Jesus, told in the books named after his disciples. In the book of Mathew, Jesus heals a paralysed man.

9 Jesus stepped into a boat, crossed over and came to his own town. ² Some men brought to him a paralyzed man, lying on a mat. When Jesus saw their faith, he said to the man, "Take heart, son; your sins are forgiven."

³ At this, some of the teachers of the law said to themselves, "This fellow is blaspheming!"

⁴ Knowing their thoughts, Jesus said, "Why do you entertain evil thoughts in your hearts? ⁵ Which is easier: to say, 'Your sins are forgiven,' or to say, 'Get up and walk'? ⁶ But I want you to know that the Son of Man has authority on earth to forgive sins." So he said to the paralyzed man, "Get up, take your mat and go home." ⁷ Then the man got up and went home. ⁸ When the crowd saw this, they were filled with awe; and they praised God, who had given such authority to man.

In Mark 6, just touching Jesus causes sensational results.

⁵³ When they had crossed over, they landed at Gennesaret and anchored there. ⁵⁴ As soon as they got out of the boat, people recognized Jesus. ⁵⁵ They ran throughout that whole region and carried the sick on mats to wherever they heard he was. ⁵⁶ And wherever he went—into villages, towns or countryside—they placed the sick in the marketplaces. They begged him to let them touch even the edge of his cloak, and all who touched it were healed.

In Luke 4, Jesus drives out a demonic spirit.

[31] *Then he went down to Capernaum, a town in Galilee, and on the Sabbath he taught the people.* [32] *They were amazed at his teaching, because his words had authority.*

[33] *In the synagogue there was a man possessed by a demon, an impure spirit. He cried out at the top of his voice,* [34] *"Go away! What do you want with us, Jesus of Nazareth? Have you come to destroy us? I know who you are—the Holy One of God!"*

[35] *"Be quiet!" Jesus said sternly. "Come out of him!" Then the demon threw the man down before them all and came out without injuring him.*

[36] *All the people were amazed and said to each other, "What words these are! With authority and power, he gives orders to impure spirits and they come out!"* [37] *And the news about him spread throughout the surrounding area.*

In John 4, an Officials' son was healed.

[43] *After the two days he left for Galilee.* [44] *(Now Jesus himself had pointed out that a prophet has no honour in his own country.)* [45] *When he arrived in Galilee, the Galileans welcomed him. They had seen all that he had done in Jerusalem at the Passover Festival, for they also had been there.*

[46] *Once more he visited Cana in Galilee, where he had turned the water into wine. And there was a certain royal official whose son lay sick at Capernaum.* [47] *When this man heard that Jesus had arrived in Galilee from Judea, he went to him and begged him to come and heal his son, who was close to death.*

[48] *"Unless you people see signs and wonders," Jesus told him, "you will never believe."*

[49] *The royal official said, "Sir, come down before my child dies."*

⁵⁰ *"Go," Jesus replied, "your son will live."*

The man took Jesus at his word and departed. ⁵¹ While he was still on the way, his servants met him with the news that his boy was living. ⁵² When he inquired as to the time when his son got better, they said to him, "Yesterday, at one in the afternoon, the fever left him."

⁵³ *Then the father realized that this was the exact time at which Jesus had said to him, "Your son will live." So he and his whole household believed.*

⁵⁴ *This was the second sign Jesus performed after coming from Judea to Galilee.*

You might be wondering why are we reading about the miracles of Jesus. Firstly, they show what is possible using the power of Jesus. Jesus carried a power to be able to heal people from sickness. Here are four cases where Jesus has used this power but there are more. There are more in the bible and there are even more that were done. John says that:

²⁵ *Jesus did many other things as well. If every one of them were written down, I suppose that even the whole world would not have room for the books that would be written.*

This means that he did an awful lot of miracles and we have less than 50 listed in the Bible. We don't know why the miracles in the bible were selected but John is suggesting a very large number of miracles and if these were book worthy miracles, they weren't small ones. I get the impression that I've missed out on a very interesting and exciting period in world history and perhaps would have benefitted from being there. On the other hand, as a born again Christian, I have the same power living in me. It's a confidence thing. Someone or something has taken my 100% confidence and replaced it with doubt and a little fear. This is the influence of the world and satan and is probably an issue with many Christians. There is also an issue where a Christian can develop so far and then settle without developing further and reaching his or her true potential. Either way, I could walk like Jesus but I don't. I get quite envious when I hear of missionary work where people go abroad and heal the blind and do other good work in the name of Jesus. Maybe my time is yet to come.

Finally, do not be waived by others, especially naysayers. Doubt or worry short circuits your faith and you do not want to be called "Ye of little faith" as in Mathew 8 where the disciples were in the fishing boat, afraid of the storm at sea.

Mathew 17 is also about faith but this time demonstrates the need of faith to perform miracles. You need faith to be miraculous and Jesus is king of this.

[14] *When they came to the crowd, a man approached Jesus and knelt before him.* [15] *"Lord, have mercy on my son," he said. "He has seizures and is suffering greatly. He often falls into the fire or into the water.* [16] *I brought him to your disciples, but they could not heal him."*

[17] *"You unbelieving and perverse generation," Jesus replied, "how long shall I stay with you? How long shall I put up with you? Bring the boy here to me."* [18] *Jesus rebuked the demon, and it came out of the boy, and he was healed at that moment.*

Everything that you need or want in this life has already been done for you so there really is no need to worry about a thing. You should be in a constant state of peace and free from unbelief or anything perverse.

∞ ∞ ∞

CHAPTER 10 Jezebel and other spirits

*O*f course we're not talking about the spirits we drink. We are talking about the spirit world and the realm in which Christians dwell. A very commonly used saying is that "Although you are in the world, you are not of it". This is very true. A Christian is a son or daughter of God and that Christian belongs in Gods world which is Heaven. John 5:19 tells us that:

We know that we are from God, and the whole world lies in the power of the evil one.

Therefore, we are citizens of heaven who live on earth but can access heavenly things until we ourselves are moved to heaven when our earthly lives end. What is interesting here is that any fruit of the spirit such as tongues, healing or prophetic ability also are left here. We don't need them in Heaven. Heaven is perfect. Therefore, if you have been given a gift, it is certainly wise to use it whilst you are on the earth.

I won't say gifts but one of our abilities is our awareness of the spiritual realm around us. All of a sudden we are aware that things aren't quite as they seem. It is a difficult situation to fully comprehend, but we are living in more than one dimension or world at the same time. They appear to be merged intricately and each can affect the other. The spirit world is as real as the physical world that we live in and now that we are in Christ, we are aware and subject to it. You might see this as good news and it is good news hence the Good News Bible. Jesus came to bring us good news. But there are opposing forces to deal with and these will test you to the limit, especially new Christians. In the book of Ephesians, we are told about them.

[12] *For our struggle is not against flesh and blood, but against the rulers, against the authorities, against the powers of this dark world and against the spiritual forces of evil in the heavenly realms.*

A soul tie is a connection that you have with another person. One of the first and a very important thing that you are advised to do when you are saved is to cut soul ties with people you know and who may spiritually influence you in the wrong direction. This might be all the people you know who serve different gods, play with evil, have been in strange relationships or just give you a feeling that something isn't right. It is so important that you keep your heart to the pure heart that you were born again with. You are advised to remove any bad influences that can spiritually corrupt you. I say spiritually because a lot of the time you won't see corruption happening. This is probably one of the reasons why Christians prefer to mingle with Christians and why we are told to marry within the faith. It is similar to buying a new pack of cards. The first thing that you do is remove the Jokers.

This is a long prayer given to me by one of the churches that I frequent and I can confirm that it does work.

Father, in the name of Jesus, I submit myself completely to You. I confess all of my emotional and sexual sins, as well as my ungodly Soul Ties. I choose to forgive each person with whom I have an ungodly Soul Tie. I ask you, Lord, to forgive me for my sin that resulted in an ungodly Soul Tie. Lord, I receive Your forgiveness. Thank you for forgiving me and for cleansing me.

I choose to forgive myself for this involvement. I will no longer be angry at myself, hate myself, or punish myself.

Lord, I break ungodly Soul Ties with _____. I release myself from them and I release them from me. As I do this, Lord, I pray that you would cause them to be all that you want them to be and that you would cause me to be all that you want me to be.

Lord, please cleanse my mind from all memories of ungodly unions so I am totally free to give myself to You and my spouse.

I renounce and cancel the assignments of all evil spirits attempting to maintain these ungodly Soul Ties.

Lord, thank you for restoring my soul to wholeness. I chose to walk in holiness by your grace.

In the name of Jesus, I pray, Amen

Even after cutting soul ties, you might just get fed up with things still going wrong? It seems that every time I go out of my way to speak about Christ, something goes wrong. In my teaching career and when I was working as a supply teacher visiting different schools, this has been my bugbear. I have openly spoken about Christ and this has done me no favours. I have in fact, learnt not to mention Jesus too often, because it makes a lot of people uncomfortable. One Muslim boy kept swearing and saying "Jesus". I did confront him and asked if he would instead say "Mohammad" but he took great offence to that. It made me realise how unimportant Jesus had been in my own life until I had become this born again man and now, Jesus is all-important. In the spirit world, there are spirits at work to make sure we don't elevate Jesus.

There is mention of quite a few demons in the bible. These are the Deaf and dumb spirit (Mark 9:17-29), Evil spirit (Luke 7:21; Acts 19:12-13), Familiar spirit (I Samuel 28:7), Foul spirit (Mark 9:25), Lying spirit (II Chronicles 18:20-22), Perverse spirit (Isaiah 19:14; Romans 1:17-32), Seducing spirit (I Timothy 4:1), Spirit of an unclean devil (Luke 4:33), Spirit of antichrist (I John 4:3), Spirit of bondage (Romans 8:15), Spirit of death (I Corinthians 10:10, 15:26), Spirit of divination (Acts 16:16), Spirit of error (I John 4:6), Spirit of fear (II Timothy 1:7), Spirit of haughtiness (Proverbs 16:18-19), Spirit of heaviness (Isaiah 61:3), Spirit of infirmity (Luke 13:11-13), Spirit of jealousy (Genesis 4:5-8; Numbers 5:14), Spirit of slumber (Isaiah 29:10, Romans 11:8), Spirit of the world (I Corinthians 2:12), Spirit of whoredom (Hosea 4:12, 5:4) and the Unclean spirit (Mark 6:7; Luke 11:24-26).

There are even more evil spirits than this in the spirit world. It's a very dark place for some. I once spoke to The Rt Revd. Stanley Elilekia Hotay, the Bishop of the Diocese of Mount Kilimanjaro in East Africa and he told me that there was quite a lot of black magic and devil worship in Africa and this was a real problem.

I once met a girl who I fell immediately in love with as if there was a force pulling me to her. I hadn't felt so good for years. I was so happy but a friend later told me that God had told him to tell me to be careful. When I went into my private place for prayer about this (a nearby Monastery), I had a clear picture of Samson and Delilah. I carried out further research and I found that there was a spirit of Delilah which is the Hebrew for "the one who weakened". This was news to me and another addition to my learning curve. I prayed and prayed about this and finally, God told me that I had been released. End of that.

Whilst looking at Delilah, I found Jezebel. Jezebel appears to be a demon of ungodly desire. Where is this in the Bible? It is in Revelation 2:20:

Nevertheless, I have this against you: You tolerate that woman Jezebel, who calls herself a prophet. By her teaching she misleads my servants into sexual immorality and the eating of food sacrificed to idols.

Jezebel is another spirit leading people away from Jesus. Just like the spirit of Ahab. This spirit is predominately focused on men who are dominated by women. You don't need to study these spirits in depth but it is always good to be aware of them especially since you can be so easily led into a sense of false comfort when you are guided by an evil spirit. If you are interested in these, then there are books available but I wanted to make you aware of what is lurking in the dark places. Not many Christians talk about these but they are real!

In my own personal journey, I had a lot of dark spiritual activity to fight with. I believe that this was because I had a previous encounter with evil. In my search to find out whether there was a God or not, I tried all sorts of things including summoning the devil. I tried to forget about that but he never did. Years later, I was driving around a roundabout late one day in the City centre near where I live and I distinctly heard "you belong to me". It took me a minute before I realised that I didn't like the sound of that. It doesn't sound very God like at all. At that point I rejected the idea in the name of Jesus Christ and declared that Jesus is my Lord and my Saviour. I know it sounds like a fairy tale story and not a particularly good one but this, to me, is living the born again life. These things can happen and do happen.

The good news is that Jesus Christ conquered the powers of evil and since we are in Jesus or Jesus is in us, then we have authority over all demonic spirit beings. You don't have to choose sides for the fight, Jesus is going to win every time. You just have to be awake or aware enough to realise that the fight is on.

Paul acknowledges that a fight is on in Ephesians 6.

[10] Finally, be strong in the Lord and in his mighty power. [11] Put on the full armour of God, so that you can take your stand against the devil's schemes. [12] For our struggle is not against flesh and blood, but against the rulers, against the authorities, against the powers of this dark world and against the spiritual forces of evil in the heavenly realms. [13] Therefore put on the full armour of God, so that when the day of evil comes, you may be able to stand your ground, and after you have done everything, to stand. [14] Stand firm

then, with the belt of truth buckled around your waist, with the breastplate of righteousness in place, ¹⁵ and with your feet fitted with the readiness that comes from the gospel of peace. ¹⁶ In addition to all this, take up the shield of faith, with which you can extinguish all the flaming arrows of the evil one. ¹⁷ Take the helmet of salvation and the sword of the Spirit, which is the word of God.

¹⁸ And pray in the Spirit on all occasions with all kinds of prayers and requests. With this in mind, be alert and always keep on praying for all the Lord's people. ¹⁹ Pray also for me, that whenever I speak, words may be given me so that I will fearlessly make known the mystery of the gospel, ²⁰ for which I am an ambassador in chains. Pray that I may declare it fearlessly, as I should.

This is a favourite of the Alpha course but not one of my favourites. This is probably because I remember having to demonstrate holding a dustpan lid and a broom or something like that. Paul, of course, is right. There is a battle going on and just as I have briefly explained, there are spiritual forces of evil at work too. The great thing is that whatever you think about the breastplate of righteousness or the belt of truth. Paul does tell us to stand firm. And this is so important. Do not be bullied because you are a son or daughter of the highest, greatest, almightiest Lord God of all time. You have the authority of Jesus and you can use it. I command you to flee, in the name of Jesus Christ. I bind you in the name of Jesus Christ. I am repeating but it is important to. Any command you give followed by "in the name of Jesus Christ" is the same as Jesus appearing right next to you and doing it himself. Christians have so much power but the devil makes sure that they don't realise it so they don't use it.

One more point to make is that Paul advises us to pray in the Spirit on all occasions. If you have the Gift of Tongues, then I suggest you use it as often as you can. It is more than just praying in a different language, there are heavenly ripples caused by it.

In the desert, Satan came after Jesus. This is told in Mathew 4.

Jesus Is Tested in the Wilderness

4 Then Jesus was led by the Spirit into the wilderness to be tempted[a] by the devil. 2 After fasting forty days and forty nights, he was hungry. 3 The tempter came to him and said, "If you are the Son of God, tell these stones to become bread."

4 Jesus answered, "It is written: 'Man shall not live on bread alone, but on every word that comes from the mouth of God."

5 Then the devil took him to the holy city and had him stand on the highest point of the temple. 6 "If you are the Son of God," he said, "throw yourself down. For it is written:

"'He will command his angels concerning you,

and they will lift you up in their hands,

so that you will not strike your foot against a stone.'"

7 Jesus answered him, "It is also written: 'Do not put the Lord your God to the test."

8 Again, the devil took him to a very high mountain and showed him all the kingdoms of the world and their splendour. 9 "All this I will give you," he said, "if you will bow down and worship me."

10 Jesus said to him, "Away from me, Satan! For it is written: 'Worship the Lord your God, and serve him only"

11 Then the devil left him, and angels came and attended him.

Another weapon that Jesus uses against satan is the word of God from the bible. Knowing your bible is another key to spiritual warfare. I have heard it said that not knowing your bible is like a sucker waiting for a punch. And it is right. You may be like me and have trouble remembering names, never mind stating what Jesus said, but it is worth doing. When I found out that I actually had the holy spirit inside of me, besides being a bit shocked, I was wondering whether I had to eat for two, like a pregnant mother. In a way you do. You eat food to survive and feed the holy spirit on the word of

God. This way, when you need the word, the holy spirit can remind you.

I suppose that I am now used to the idea of being in this spiritual warfare and I am used to the concept of spirits, both good and bad. I am used to the fact that evils spirits or demons are working against me, trying to make me stumble as I walk the Christian path. I am getting used to loosing things of God and binding the things of Satan. I am getting used to shouting at the devil in my car and clapping my hands in rejection. I am also getting used to praying and talking to my invisible best friend called Jesus. Here I take a moment for you to think about this.

You too might be the same but be aware that this can seem very strange to the natural world around you. I spoke to a psychiatrist I once met. We spoke at length about Christianity and living the Christian life. I was fully open with him and he very much agreed with me. He told me that he too had a client that was hearing voices. He also told me that he was in secure accommodation out of society and that, whether these voices are true or not, I should be careful to whom I talk to, lest they try and lock me away also. This is the terrible reality of society today. No matter how true all this is, there are plenty of people who can't see it. The spirit world is real. Jesus is real. However, beware of who you tell. Not everybody loves Jesus and in fact, it can be quite the opposite. Many didn't like Jesus when he was here so please don't assume that they're going to like you.

Jesus doesn't tell us to be as shrewd as snakes and as innocent as doves (Mathew 16) for no reason. The devil can imitate anything he wants and he can provide anything he wants just as he offered the whole world to Jesus when Jesus was being tempted in the desert. Have you ever bought a fake product that doesn't last very long? The devil is all about fake and believe me, anything he offers isn't going to last long. Of course, Jesuhe tols could easily figure him out with his false promises and kept his heart and mind set on the things of heaven. This is what we should also do.

∞ ∞ ∞

CHAPTER 11 *God given gifts*

*A*s I mentioned earlier, the devil is a master of trickery and deceit. He can give you what you want but this won't last.

I find it interesting how with the many people alive today are searching for the father and are tricked into finding him in places other than the bible. Many people have experienced a sensation that they say is heavenly through the use of drugs. I spoke to an ex heroin addict who was on the methadone program (substitute drug). He told me never to try heroin and he told me that there are different strengths of heroin so is possible that people could have heaven-like experiences. He described his experiences and he told me that if he is sitting with a cup of tea watching TV, then he is sitting in the best chair in the world, drinking the best tea in the world and watching the best TV in the world. I had to think that that sounded heavenly to me!

Smoking cannabis or weed can instantly remove any worries or problems and give you a sense of peace which is inferior but similar to the peace of the Lord and temporary. Because it is temporary, this also tells you that it is nothing to do with Jesus. Unfortunately, some drug users can spend the rest of their lives chasing sensations but never attaining the glory that us Christians can bask in. And it is in vain, because the real heaven is not through drugs but through Jesus.

You don't need to take drugs or anything else to know that your Father in Heaven loves you and that you will be with him, one day.

In the meantime, we have the Holy Spirit and the Gifts of the holy spirit, some of which I've witnessed first-hand.

In 1 Corinthians 12, we read that:

Now about the gifts of the Spirit, brothers and sisters, I do not want you to be uninformed. 2 You know that when you were pagans, somehow or other you were influenced and led astray to mute idols. 3 Therefore I want you to know that no one who is speaking by the Spirit of God says, "Jesus be cursed," and no one can say, "Jesus is Lord," except by the Holy Spirit.

4 There are different kinds of gifts, but the same Spirit distributes them. 5 There are different kinds of service, but the same Lord. 6 There are different kinds of working, but in all of them and in everyone it is the same God at work.

7 Now to each one the manifestation of the Spirit is given for the common good. 8 To one there is given through the Spirit a message of wisdom, to another a message of knowledge by means of the same Spirit, 9 to another faith by the same Spirit, to another gifts of healing by that one Spirit, 10 to another miraculous powers, to another prophecy, to another distinguishing between spirits, to another speaking in different kinds of tongues, and to still another the interpretation of tongues. 11 All these are the work of one and the same Spirit, and he distributes them to each one, just as he determines.

Here we can be absolutely sure that the Holy Spirit gives gifts to Christians and not just Jesus. So you might have one, all or some of the gifts that the Bible talks about and are absolutely true and available today. I can testify to this because of my own experiences.

As I have already discussed, I received the **gift of tongues** about two years after being born again. I speak in ancient Hebrew whenever I like and I am worshipping the Father as I do. If I can't think of what to pray or I need urgent assistance, I switch to tongues. In 1 Corinthians 14, Paul wishes that all Christians would speak in tongues which certainly suggests that not everybody did.

Follow the way of love and eagerly desire gifts of the Spirit, especially prophecy. ² For anyone who speaks in a tongue does not speak to people but to God. Indeed, no one understands them; they utter mysteries by the Spirit. ³ But the one who prophesies speaks to people for their strengthening, encouraging and comfort. ⁴ Anyone who speaks in a tongue edifies themselves, but the one who prophesies edifies the church. ⁵ I would like every one of you to speak in tongues, but I would rather have you prophesy. The one who prophesies is greater than the one who speaks in tongues, unless someone interprets, so that the church may be edified.

Here we see another gift which is the **gift of prophecy**. Prophecy is pretty much a prediction of what will happen in the future. You may recall that in Chapter 9, I had a vision of two people on the train which was prophecy about the change in leadership in my local church. There are many people who have the gift of prophecy and the prophets that I know, always hear God and have messages for other people. We have a prophet in our local church but I will confess that I don't always understand him. I also went on a Prophetic training course where we practiced listening to the spirit and allowed pictures to form in our minds. All because of the Holy Spirit of course. There are prophets in the Bible too. Probably my favourite is Isaiah because of his immaculate predictions of Jesus and especially that of Isaiah 53 which describes Jesus many lifetimes before he existed.

⁴ Surely he took up our pain
and bore our suffering,
yet we considered him punished by God,
stricken by him, and afflicted.
⁵ But he was pierced for our transgressions,
he was crushed for our iniquities;
the punishment that brought us peace was on him,
and by his wounds we are healed.
⁶ We all, like sheep, have gone astray,

each of us has turned to our own way;
and the Lord *has laid on him*
  the iniquity of us all.

It is also interesting to note that in the Bible there are major prophets and minor prophets. This doesn't mean that some prophets are "hit and miss" and others are "spot on". It means that the books of the Prophets are long or are short. They are major or minor.

Another gift is described as a message of knowledge. This I know as a **word of knowledge**. My friend had told me that people have come to him and told him that they have a word of knowledge for him which is essentially a word from God via another person. Bizarre, I thought. Shortly after, and on my own Christian journey, I was struggling to understand the relationship between the Church of England and the Catholic Church and was concerned that I was born again into the Church of England and my daughter was attending a Catholic school with their own doctrines or beliefs. Typically, I was in church on Sunday when a gentleman approached me. He told me that I didn't know him and that he felt he had a word from the Lord for me. He then told me how he saw what seemed like the Vatican with Gods light and presence shining into it. He told me he didn't know what it meant but I had a fairly good idea. How amazing is that? The almighty God of the universe sending someone to me with my very own personal message.

Chapter 9 gives mention of the **gift of healing** and it just remains to say that it is fantastic that this is going on today. I just wish that Christians were less shy and that Christian healings even made the news. I have healed some people but then again I haven't. It is God who heals and sometimes He heals through me and more often than not He doesn't. God decides whether to heal or not, all we can do is ask by commanding in Jesus's name. I also think it takes a lot of courage to stand out and say, actually I'm a Christian and I can heal. You automatically think they're going to think that you are a nutter and now you are wondering whether you should have said anything in the first place. Boldness is required as is confidence that what you do will work. The key to this is to be expectant. Expect results from your healing hands and there is every chance that you will see them.

There is also the **gift of discernment** which is the ability to recognise and determine what spirit is at work and where. Not everybody will encounter Jezebel, but there are plenty of other dodgy spirits and if things are going wrong, there's usually a spirit lurking somewhere.

This gives you an idea of what the Christian can expect to operate in and with. Remember that before you were born of the spirit, none of this mattered. Now it is very important and if there is a particular gift you desire (perhaps something I haven't even mentioned), you can always ask.

What is even more important is that if you have a gift, you must use it whilst you are on earth because there are no "gifts" in Heaven.

∞ ∞ ∞

CHAPTER 12 *Peace of the Lord*

*T*here is not a Christian on earth that doesn't want to go to Heaven. And I'm happy to bet that there are also no Christians in Heaven that want to go to earth. Christians do, however, have a taste of Heaven on this earth.

Basically put, heaven is a copy of earth but there is no evil, wrong doing or anything that disturbs the peace. There are no weapons or police because there is no need for them. Heaven is heaven. It is idyllic and peaceful and although I have said that it is a copy of earth, it is not an exact copy of earth. I understand that your senses are multiplied, your feelings are exaggerated and your vision is magnified. Everything is much better and improved on what we have got. Jesus, coming down from heaven to earth, must have expected a rough deal just by looking at the place.

In Dr Eben Alexanders' book, "Proof of Heaven", I loved to read that he could hear the flapping of the butterfly's wings. That is superb. I myself have witnessed the prince like man riding on a horse and have asked many Christians about their experiences. You might like to find your most beautiful scenery painting with the sun shining and the river flowing by the spring time fields with pink and white blossom blowing in the warm breeze. It's a bit like that too. Heaven is like earth but is much better. Of course this is a simplistic view of where we will be living. In his next book, "The Map of Heaven", he explains that to go to heaven or to experience heaven, you need to be spiritually attuned to it and that the purer you become, the more able you are to access this. Similarly, Jesus is the pinnacle of purity.

There is no sin. Sin stays on the earth. In heaven you cannot sin because sinful thoughts cannot cross your mind because sin doesn't exist. Heaven is purely good, which we can say by removing just one "o", Heaven is purely God.

In John 14, Jesus comforts his disciples about where he is going.

"Do not let your hearts be troubled. You believe in God; believe also in me. ² My Father's house has many rooms; if that were not so, would I have told you that I am going there to prepare a place for you? ³ And if I go and prepare a place for you, I will come back and take you to be with me that you also may be where I am. ⁴ You know the way to the place where I am going."

I love the thought that we have somewhere to go when we die. I love to think that people I know and knew will be there or at least I hope so. I already have a few questions stored up for Moses and Jesus. They will be there, no matter how far-fetched it seems. I'm hoping my dad and my grandparents are too. But what is important is that I use the time I have left on earth to make sure the rest of my family come to Christ at the very least. You should not be thinking of who you can live without but you should be thinking about who you can get in and live with.

I don't see it as anybody's fault that don't know God. They are taken away from God by the world around us, a world ruled by satan or the devil. Notice that I never use capitals for satan or the devil because I am now in a place where they are not even worthy of namely recognition. I am in Gods Rest which is where I am trusting in Him for everything in my life.

Our God is greater, our God is bigger and our Gsadiod is much more worthy of worship and admiration and love and joy. No wonder people were overjoyed when Jesus arrived. If there was a popularity contest, he'd have won hands down. That's what the authorities were scared of and that's what got him killed.

Jesus is also known as the Prince of Peace. The amazing thing is that he got the name hundreds of years before he was born. It was the prophet Isaiah in the Old Testament.

"For to us a child is born, to us a son is given, and the government will be on his shoulders. And he will be called Wonderful Counsellor, Mighty God, Everlasting Father, **Prince of Peace.***"*

What is interesting is that God is all about peace. His kingdom is all about peace. And being a Christian is all about peace. Giving your problems to God relieves your mind from worry and doubt and trouble and leaves you free for the peace. A very important point to make here is that once you have given your problem or problems to God, it is not recommended that you take it back. If you have entrusted God with a problem that you have and asked Him to help, it effectively becomes His problem. You must let go of it. If you continue to think about it and worry about it then this is taking the problem back and once again it becomes your problem. It is best not to do this.

In the Pentecostal church they have a part of the service where they sometimes lay hands on each other and fall in the spirit. You may have seen this on the television or read about it in books. It is also known as Slain in the spirit. I was keen to try it and people prayed over me in tongues and I fell, but instead of hurting myself, it was a soft fall and then I lay on the ground with a peace second to none. Evaporation of any worries or worldly thoughts, just peace and reluctance to do anything other than bask in it. It was great. I realised that this is what Jesus was talking about when he spoke about the peace that passes all understanding. It was beautiful. I couldn't wait to do it again and if this is what heaven is like, then I'm in the queue.

There's not many people who have been to a Church of England church and not said "The peace of the Lord be with you" or something very similar. John 14 tells us that Jesus really does promote peace.

*"**Peace** I leave with you; my **peace** I give you. I do not give to you as the world gives. Do not let your hearts be troubled and do not be afraid".*

Paul, in his letter to the Ephesians tells us more about what Jesus did.

*"He came and preached **peace** to you who were far away and **peace** to those who were near".*

There are over 200 references to "peace" in the Bible and this is because Jesus's message is to take us away from sin and misbehaviour and take us into a world of peace and harmony and gentleness and kindness and love. This is what I call heaven and because of Jesus, it starts here on earth and continues into eternity.

I Peter 4 advises us that we are finished with our sinful nature and are now to serve God.

Therefore, since Christ suffered in his body, arm yourselves also with the same attitude, because whoever suffers in the body is done with sin. [2] As a result, they do not live the rest of their earthly lives for evil human desires, but rather for the will of God.

Presence is similar to peace but presence is when the lord our God is with us. They are both very special and very Christian things. You might think that you have peace at night when all the doors are locked and you are snug in bed in silence. Well, that is a type of peace but the peace that we are talking about is peace in your heart and mind which is a stillness, there's no wrestling thoughts or worries, just peace.   The presence is taking this peace a step further. The presence is often felt when you are with another Christian who is born again and this is when I have experienced it. Matthew 18 tells us this.

[19] *"Again, truly I tell you that if two of you on earth agree about anything they ask for, it will be done for them by my Father in heaven.* [20] *For where two or three gather in my name, there am I with them."*

Presence is a change in the atmosphere to almost an atmosphere of love. You don't necessarily love the other Christian that you are with but the air is full of a thickness of love and you just know that God is present with you. Often you cannot resist but to speak or sing worship and in tongues if possible. It really is magical and quite often it can be a result of summoning the spirit where you ask the spirit to come.

While we are on earth, we have something called our "calling". Simply put, this is what God has decided that we will do with our lives and for him. For some it may be to pray for others and for some it may be full-time ministry. Only God knows what his plans are for us and He only tells us when he is ready and not before. Jeremiah tells us that they are good plans.

"For I know the plans I have for you," declares the LORD, "plans to prosper you and not to harm you, plans to give you hope and a future. [12] *Then you will call on me and come and pray to me, and I will listen to you.* [13] *You will seek me and find me when you seek me with all your heart. "*

What a waste of time it is spending this precious life you have chasing money and all the luxuries that it can buy. These are all temporary and they are of the earth and will remain on the earth when you die. We could all die tomorrow since we all have a last day and therefore time well spent would be time with Jesus and investing your energy in doing good works for his kingdom. As you get older, you will find that the days tend to disappear quicker than they did when you were young. You don't need to be in a hurry to be in Heaven because it will happen soon enough.

Give your full life to Christ as he gave his life for you. He did not pay the price with his life so that he could have a few hours of you on a Sunday but he paid for all of you, all of the time. Give all to

Christ and allow yourself to be led by the spirit and enjoy your journey. You know that you will eventually be in the best and most peaceful place you will ever go. There is no other place like it. Heaven is waiting and it's waiting for you.

But blessed is the one who trusts in the LORD,
whose confidence is in him.

Jeremiah 17

Printed in Great
Britain
by Amazon